Windows® 11
For Seniors

Windows® 11 For Seniors

2nd Edition

by Curt Simmons

A Wiley Brand

Windows® 11 For Seniors For Dummies®, 2nd Edition

Published by: **John Wiley & Sons, Inc.,** 111 River Street, Hoboken, NJ 07030-5774, www.wiley.com

For general information on our other products and services, please contact our Customer Care Department within the U.S. at 877-762-2974, outside the U.S. at 317-572-3993, or fax 317-572-4002. For technical support, please visit https://hub.wiley.com/community/support/dummies.

Wiley publishes in a variety of print and electronic formats and by print-on-demand. Some material included with standard print versions of this book may not be included in e-books or in print-on-demand. If this book refers to media that is not included in the version you purchased, you may download this material at http://booksupport.wiley.com. For more information about Wiley products, visit www.wiley.com.

Library of Congress Control Number: 2024951613

ISBN 978-1-394-27691-2 (pbk); ISBN 978-1-394-27693-6 (ebk); ISBN 978-1-394-27692-9 (ebk)

SKY10093530_121224

Contents at a Glance

Table of Contents

Introduction

Windows 11 is the latest generation of Microsoft's operating system, the master program that makes a computer useful and provides support to other programs, including word processors, photo viewers, and web browsers. Much as an education equips you to read a novel or play a game, Windows 11 equips your computer to perform a wide range of activities. You can use Windows 11 and other software (or *apps*) to read or write a novel, play games or music, and stay in touch with friends and family around the world.

As Windows has evolved over the past 40 years, so have computers — the *hardware*. Today, you can buy a computer as small as a watch, and even such a little computer is unimaginably more powerful than (and a fraction of the cost of) computers just 10 years ago.

You don't need much time with a computer to conclude that there has to be an easier way to do things. At times, computers seem overly complex and inscrutable. Have you used a smartphone lately? Or a TV remote control? Why are the controls on every microwave oven different? Why does every new tool offer countless options you don't want that obscure the ones you do want? Well, I don't have the answers to those questions, but I do have step-by-step instructions for many tasks you want to perform using Windows 11.

After many years of working with computers, I find that they reward patience, curiosity, and a little methodical exploration. Seniors, in particular, know that learning never really stops and that learning new things keeps one young, at least figuratively. By the end of this book, you may be a multitasking computerist performing virtual gymnastics with Windows 11. On the other hand, if this book helps you do only one thing — use email, browse the web, or enjoy photos or music — that one useful thing may be all you need.

About This Book

Age is just a number. This book is intended for anyone getting started with Windows 11 who wants step-by-step instructions without a lot of discussion. Numerous figures with notes show you the computer screen as you progress through the steps. Reading this book is like having an experienced friend stand behind you as you use Windows 11 . . . someone who never takes control of the computer away from you.

Windows 11 is a work in progress. Microsoft updates the Windows 11 operating system from time to time to make it more secure and agreeable to the people who use it. (Chapter 3 explains how to check for updates to Windows 11.) Because the operating system is continuously updated, the screen shots you see in this book may not exactly match what you see on your screen.

Conventions Used in This Book

This book uses certain conventions to highlight important information and help you find your way around:

» **Different methods for performing steps:** In general, you can complete a step in three ways. I list the choices as follows:

   • **Mouse:** If you have a mouse, follow these instructions.

   • **Touchscreen:** You may be able to touch your screen to perform tasks.

   • **Keyboard:** Keyboard shortcuts are often the fastest way to do something.

   When you have a choice between these methods, experiment to determine which is easiest for you.

» **Tip icons:** These point out helpful suggestions related to tasks in the step lists.

» **Bold:** I use bold for figure references as well as for when you have to type something onscreen using the keyboard.

TIP

Many figures have notes or other markings to draw your attention to a specific part of the figure. The text tells you what to look for; the figure notes help you find it.

» **Website addresses:** If you bought an e-book, website addresses are live links. In the text, website addresses look like this: www.dummies.com. See Chapter 6 for information on browsing the web.

» **Options and buttons:** Although Windows 11 often uses lowercase in option and button names, I capitalize the text for emphasis. That way, you can find a button labeled Save Now, even though onscreen it appears as *Save now*.

How to Read This Book

You can work through this book from beginning to end or simply look at the table of contents or index to find the instructions you need to solve a problem or learn a new skill whenever you need it. The steps in each task get you where you want to go quickly, without a lot of technical explanation. In no time, you'll start picking up the skills you need to become a confident Windows 11 user.

Technology always comes with its own terms and concepts, but you don't need to learn another language to use a computer. You don't need any prior experience with computers or Windows. Step-by-step instructions guide you through specific tasks, such as accessing the news or playing a game. These steps provide just the information you need for the task at hand.

Foolish Assumptions

We assume that you have a computer and want clear, brief, step-by-step instructions on getting things done with Windows 11. I assume also that you want to know only what you need to know, just when you need to know it. This isn't Computers 101. This is Practical

Windows 11. As an old friend said, "I don't want to make a watch; I just want to know what time it is."

How This Book Is Organized

This book is divided into four parts to help you find what you need. You can read from cover to cover or just jump to the page that interests you.

» **Part 1: Getting Started with Windows 11:** In Chapter 1, you turn on the computer and get comfortable with essential parts of Windows 11, such as the Start screen, as well as how to use a mouse, touchscreen, or keyboard. Explore features of Windows 11 apps in Chapter 2, including Copilot AI. To customize Windows 11 to work better for you, turn to Chapter 3. In Chapter 4, you create and modify user account settings, such as passwords. You discover the desktop, how to manage windows, and how to customize the desktop in Chapter 5.

» **Part 2: Windows 11 and the Web:** Use the web to stay current and keep in touch. Turn to Chapter 6 to use Edge to browse the web. Send and receive email in Chapter 7. Stay in touch with friends and family with Microsoft Teams in Chapter 8. Turn to Chapter 9 to explore a handful of apps that can help you stay in touch with friends and get to know the outside world better.

» **Part 3: Having Fun with Windows 11:** If you haven't been having any fun until now, I've failed you. Expand your tools and toys in Chapter 10 by connecting to Microsoft Store to install new apps. In Chapter 11, you enjoy photos on Windows 11 and put your own photos on the computer. If you want to listen to music and watch a video, see Chapter 12.

» **Part 4: Beyond the Basics:** In Chapter 13, you learn about the care and feeding of Windows 11, which requires a little maintenance now and then. Find out how to connect a printer and other hardware, such as a mouse and a second screen, in Chapter 14. Do you appreciate the saying "a place for everything and everything in its place"? Chapter 15 is where you find out how to organize your documents. And finally, you back up your files to ensure against loss and refresh Windows 11 when it gets cranky in Chapter 16.

Beyond the Book

In addition to what you're reading right now, this book comes with a free, access-anywhere Cheat Sheet that helps you search the web without a browser, quickly locate recently used files from the Start screen, view file extensions in File Explorer, and take a screen-shot. To get this Cheat Sheet, simply go to www.dummies.com and type **Windows 11 For Seniors For Dummies Cheat Sheet** into the Search box.

1

Getting Started with Windows 11

Chapter **1**

Getting Acquainted with Windows 11

Windows 11 is an *operating system* (the master program for any computer). You can use Windows 11 on a wide range of devices, from a smartphone to a big-screen TV/ entertainment system: One size fits most. You can not only use the same programs with a range of hardware but also access the documents you create (such as photos and email — files and data, to nerds) from any Windows-based computer, giving you extraordinary freedom of choice and mobility.

Although countless companies create programs you may use, Microsoft attempts to make similar functions consistent across different programs. For example, opening a document or emailing a photo to a friend involves the same steps regardless of the programs you use. You don't have to learn a different way of doing common tasks in each program. This consistency will serve you well when using Windows 11 and other new programs.

In this chapter, you start your computer and work with the *Start screen*, the dashboard for Windows 11. You explore options for using the Start screen with your *hardware* (the computer and related devices). Then you exit Windows 11 and go right back in for more.

The easiest way to get Windows 11 is preinstalled on a new computer. If your current computer runs an older version of Windows (such as Windows 10), you can upgrade to Windows 11 for free, although older machines may lack newer functions, such as a touchscreen, and may have some hardware compatibility problems with Windows 11 as well. Visit microsoft.com for details about upgrading from an older operating system.

Tell Your Computer What to Do

How do you get Windows 11 to do what you want it to do? You can command a computer in many ways, depending on your equipment (hardware). For example, a desktop computer has different options from a handheld phone. You may have any or all of these choices:

» Mouse

» Touchscreen

» Keyboard

Another device for controlling Windows is a touchpad, which is commonly found on a laptop keyboard. You move your finger on the touchpad to move the pointer on the screen.

A desktop computer keyboard and mouse may be wired (they plug into the computer) or they may be wireless (no wires needed!). Don't like the keyboard or mouse that came with your desktop computer? You can purchase many different styles and connect a new one to your Windows 11 PC. Shop wherever computers and related equipment are sold.

If you have a computer with more than one of these devices, you might use one device exclusively or, more likely, vary your choice according to the task. Use whichever technique is easiest for you, but don't be afraid to experiment. In the next few sections, you discover the ins and outs of using all these methods of controlling Windows 11. Then you're ready to turn on your computer and use these methods.

In the steps throughout this book, *choose* or *select* refers to using a mouse, the touchscreen, or a physical keyboard. *Drag* refers to using a mouse or a finger.

Move the Mouse

A *mouse* is a soap–bar–sized device that you move across a desk with your hand. Move the mouse and note how the arrow called a *mouse pointer* moves across the computer screen. (Similar to a mouse, a *trackball* is a ball in a socket that you can rotate to move the mouse pointer.) A mouse has two or more buttons; some also have a scroll wheel between the buttons.

The following terms describe methods for using a mouse with Windows 11. In each, move the mouse first to position the pointer over a specified item before proceeding:

» **Click:** Move the onscreen arrow-shaped mouse pointer over a specified item and press and release the left mouse button: That's a click (sometimes called a left-click to distinguish it from a right-click).

» **Right-click:** Press and release the right mouse button to display available functions. Note that the word *click* by itself means use the left mouse button.

» **Drag:** Press and hold down the left mouse button, and then move the mouse pointer across the screen. When you want to move an object, you drag it. Release the mouse button to release the object.

Watch for the word *click* to indicate using a mouse button and *scroll* to indicate using the mouse wheel.

Touch the Screen

A *touchscreen*, as the name says, enables you to touch the screen to tell your computer what to do. You typically use one finger or two, although touchscreens may allow you to use all ten digits. In some cases, you can also use a special pen called a *stylus* instead of your finger. Tablet computers and some smartphones have touchscreens. Touchscreens are less common on desktop or laptop computers, but that situation is changing. Not sure what type of screen you have? When you have Windows 11 running, lightly slide your index finger up or down on the screen to see what happens.

The following terms refer to ways you interact with a touchscreen:

» **Tap:** Briefly touch the screen. You *select* an object, such as a button, by tapping it.

» **Drag:** Touch and hold your finger on the screen, then move your finger across the screen. You *move* an object, such as an onscreen playing card, by dragging it.

» **Swipe:** Touch and move your finger more quickly than with drag. You can swipe your finger across the screen from any of the four sides of the screen to display options and commands. You swipe pages to move forward or back. You may see the word *flick* instead of *swipe.* Some people insist that a flick is faster or shorter than a swipe, but you don't need to get caught up in that debate.

» **Pinch and unpinch:** Touch a finger and thumb or two fingers on the screen. Move your fingers closer to each other to *pinch* and away from each other to *unpinch.* Generally, a pinch reduces the size of something on the screen or shows more content on the screen. An unpinch (an ugly word) *zooms in,* increasing the size of something onscreen to show more detail.

TIP

Watch for the words *tap, swipe,* or *pinch* to indicate using your finger. Touch actions are often called *gestures.*

See the upcoming section "View the Touch Keyboard" if your computer doesn't have a physical keyboard, as is often the case with a touchscreen.

Use a Keyboard

A typewriter-like keyboard is a traditional device for controlling a computer and is especially useful when you must enter a lot of text. Special key combinations, called *shortcut keys,* are often the quickest way to do anything (though they require some memorization).

The following keys are particularly noteworthy. No offense intended to fans of keys not noted here. Although you won't use all these keys immediately, you'll find it helpful to locate each one on your keyboard.

Press indicates that you use the keyboard (physical or virtual) for the specified key or sequence of keys (just as *click* indicates a mouse action and *tap* indicates touching the screen). Combinations of keys are not pressed simultaneously. Instead, press and hold the first key in the specified sequence, press the second key, and then release both. (I explain exceptions to this method as necessary.)

>> ⌘: Called the Windows key, this key is usually located on either side of the spacebar, which is the largest key. ⌘ works by itself, as you'll soon see, as well as in combination with many other keys. Throughout the book, I specify these combinations where you might use them. There will be a quiz later. (Kidding! No quizzes.)

>> **Tab:** Press the Tab key to select an item on a window, dialog box, or even web page. Press Tab repeatedly to skip items you don't intend to select.

The keyboard can be used to select objects but is less direct than using touch or a mouse.

- » **Arrow keys:** Press the arrow keys to move the cursor or selection of an object in the direction the keys point (left, right, up, or down). In some contexts, Tab and the right arrow do the same thing. Sorry to be vague, but context matters at times.

- » **Enter:** In most cases, the Enter key on the keyboard chooses a selection, much as clicking or tapping does. However, you may need to use the Tab key or an arrow key to select an item before pressing the Enter key.

- » **Ctrl, Alt,** and **Shift keys:** These keys are used with other keys for commands. For example, press Ctrl+C to copy selected text or an object. (That is, while pressing and holding down the Ctrl key, press the C key — no need to press Shift for an uppercase C. Then release both keys.) The Shift key is used with another key for uppercase.

- » **Backspace:** As you enter text, each press of Backspace erases the character to the left of the cursor.

- » **Delete:** As you enter text, each press of the Delete key erases the character to the right of the cursor. On some keyboards, this key is labeled Del.

- » **Function keys:** All keys function, but Function keys are labeled F1 through F12. You don't use these much in this book, but you should locate them. Laptops often have a separate Function Lock key to turn these keys on or off.

- » **Page keys:** Locate the Home, End, Page Up, and Page Down keys for future reference. Use these to move the screen, a page, or the cursor. (On some keyboards, the Home, End, Page Up, and Page Down keys work as numbers when the Num Lock key is activated.)

View the Touch Keyboard

Windows 11 can display a touch keyboard onscreen. This feature is vital for devices that have a touchscreen and no physical keyboard. With a touchscreen, the touch keyboard appears automatically when the *cursor* (a blinking vertical bar) indicates that you can enter text in a box. If the touch keyboard doesn't appear automatically, you may also see a separate box floating above or below the text box. Tap that floating box to display the keyboard. Or, if you don't see a floating keyboard, tap the keyboard icon on the taskbar to the right (it's close to the date and time). To type using the keyboard, simply tap or click a letter, number, or symbol key.

TIP

Here are the different types of touch keyboards:

» The *standard layout* (also called QWERTY) appears automatically (see **Figure 1-1**). The Enter key changes depending on the context.

» The *uppercase layout,* shown in **Figure 1-2**, appears when you tap the Shift key on the standard layout.

Settings

Emojis

Close

FIGURE 1-1

FIGURE 1-2

- » The *numbers and symbols layout* appears when you tap the &123 key on the standard layout. Tap the &123 key again to return to the standard layout.

- » The control keys overlay appears on five keys on the standard layout when you tap the Ctrl key. The Ctrl keys are used in common tasks, such as copying (Ctrl+C) or moving (Ctrl+X) selected text. The overlay disappears automatically after you tap one of the control keys (A, Z, X, C, or V).

- » Select the Settings button (refer to **Figure 1-1**). The Setting button appears on the top left of the touch keyboard (it looks like a gear). Here, you can select the Keyboard Layout. Default is selected automatically, but you can choose Small, Split, or Traditional. You can also choose to switch to a Handwriting option, which lets you write with your finger. Windows converts your scribbles to block text. Finally, you can also select Theme and Resize. This opens the Personalization window, where you can select different keyboard and size options, shown in **Figure 1-3**.

FIGURE 1-3

» Finally, you can add emoticons as you type. Select the emojis button (refer to Figure 1-1) and touch or search for the emoticon you want to use.

Turn On Your Computer

1. Push the power button briefly and release it. Every computer has a power button. (When we can no longer turn them off, the machines win.) If you have a desktop computer tower, the power button is probably on the front of the tower. Otherwise, you may have to feel around the front and sides of the screen or near the hinges of a laptop. Typically, your computer will beep, some buttons will light, and the screen may flash a logo or message that disappears before you can read it. (Just let that go.) Soon, you will see the Windows 11 Lock screen.

2. Turn on any separate hardware (such as a monitor, speakers, or a printer), if necessary.

3. Enter your password and press Enter (or select the Submit button, the button on the right side of the password textbox). Soon the Windows 11 desktop screen appears, as shown in **Figure 1-4**.

TIP

You may be able to log in using your fingerprint or even facial recognition to sign-in, depending on your computer's features. You can check by using the Search box and taskbar. Search for Settings and then choose Accounts ⇨ Sign-in Options. If you can use a sign-in method other than a password, you'll see the options here.

TIP

If you don't see the Password text box, jiggle the mouse or press a key on the keyboard to wake up Windows 11.

TIP

The first time you turn on a new computer, a series of Windows Setup screens appears. Accept the defaults or change them appropriately and then select the button labeled Next.

FIGURE 1-4

TIP

If your computer doesn't have a keyboard, as is the case with many tablet computers, see the preceding section, "View the Touch Keyboard," for information on how to type onscreen.

TIP

If this is the first time that Windows 11 has started on your computer, you must create a user account, even if no one else will use the machine. See Chapter 4 for details on creating and changing user accounts.

Check Out the Start Screen

1. Start your computer — if it isn't started already — and sign in to your user account. You see the Windows desktop screen (refer to **Figure 1-4**).

2. Open the Start screen, as shown in **Figure 1-5**. Use one of these methods to open the Start screen:

Apps

All Apps button

Pinned   All apps >

Edge	Word	Excel	PowerPoint	Microsoft 365 (Office)	Outlook (new)
Microsoft Store	Photos	Vantage	User Guide	Settings	Xbox
Solitaire & Casual Games	Spotify	Paint	Microsoft Clipchamp	LinkedIn	Calculator

← Next Page button

Recommended   More >

Skype
Recently added

Maps
Recently added

9781394276912 fg0103
6m ago

Screenshot 2024-08-28 120817
6m ago

ES_Through the Woods · Erik Fernh...
58m ago

ES_Hiding in the Woods · Eoin Ma...
59m ago

Curt Simmons

← Power

Account   **Recommended section and More button**

FIGURE 1-5

- **Mouse:** Click the Start button (you find it on the taskbar, which is the strip across the bottom of the screen). The Start button is the leftmost icon on the taskbar; it looks like a four-pane window.

- **Touchscreen:** Tap the Start button.

- **Keyboard:** Press the ⌘ key.

3. Examine the Start screen and note the icons. These icons represent available *apps* (short for application programs, an older term for programs or software). By clicking or tapping an app icon, you can open an app. (See Chapter 2 for information on using individual apps.)

4. You can take a look at more apps by clicking the Next Page button (refer to **Figure 1-5**). Also, you can see an alphabetical list of all the

apps that are installed on your computer, as shown in **Figure 1-6**, by clicking the All Apps button (refer to **Figure 1-5**). By clicking or tapping an app in this list, you can open an app. Click the Back button to go back to the main Start Screen page.

Under Recommended, you see recent files that you've opened. Click More to see a complete list. This is a handy way to find a file you recently used.

While the Start screen is open, you can type the name of an app to open it. For example, to open the Weather app, type **weather**. This automatically changes the Start screen to the Search screen, which you can also open directly by clicking the Search icon on the task-bar. Select the Weather app listing in the search results to open the Weather app.

FIGURE 1-6

TIP

Rather than scroll through the alphabetical list to find an app, you can select a letter in the list and then select a letter in the pop-up list of letters that appears (refer to **Figure 1-7**). For example, to quickly get to the Weather app, select any letter and then select the W on the pop-up list.

5. Click or tap your image (or image and name) on the Start screen. As shown in **Figure 1-8**, you see a pop-up menu with commands for accessing your account settings (see Chapter 3) or signing out in a favor of another person who shares your computer (see Chapter 4). Who would think that clicking your name would open a pop-up menu?

&	#	A	B
C	D	E	F
G	H	I	J
K	L	M	N
O	P	Q	R
S	T	U	V
W	X	Y	Z

Q Search for apps, settings, and documents

All apps   ‹ Back

⊕

Curt Simmons   ⏻

FIGURE 1-7

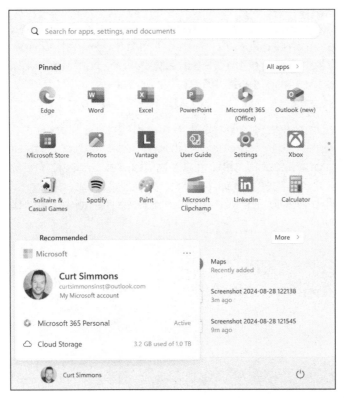

FIGURE 1-8

6. Click or tap Power on the Start menu. As shown in **Figure 1-9**, you see a pop-up menu with commands for putting your computer to sleep, shutting down your computer, and restarting your computer. Later in this chapter, "Shut Down Your Computer" looks into the options on this pop-up menu.

7. Click or tap the Start button. Doing any of these actions when the Start screen is open closes the Start screen. You can also close the Start screen by clicking anywhere on the desktop when the Start screen is open.

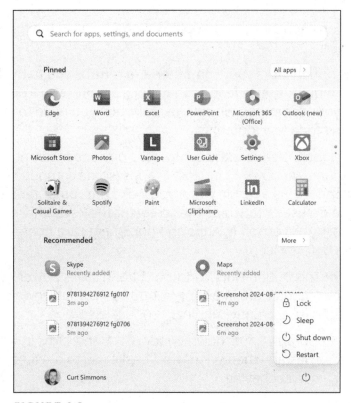

FIGURE 1-9

Shut Down Your Computer

1. When you have finished using your computer for a while, you may want to shut down Windows 11. Begin by displaying the Start screen:

   - **Mouse:** Click the Start button on the taskbar. The Start button is the leftmost icon and looks like a four-pane window.

   - **Touchscreen:** Tap the Start button.

   - **Keyboard:** Press the ⌘ key.

2. Click or tap Power on the Start menu (refer to **Figure 1-9**). The Power button is on the bottom right side of the Start menu and looks like a circle with a line through the top.

3. Available options appear in a pop-up box. Some or all of the following options appear:

- **Lock:** This option locks your computer and returns you to the login screen. It's a quick-to-use feature that stops anyone else from accessing your computer, which is useful when you need to step away from it for a few moments.

- **Sleep:** This option reduces the computer's power consumption without exiting Windows 11 or closing apps (some computers don't offer this option). As a result, when you wake the computer by moving the mouse or touching the screen or the keyboard, everything is exactly as you left it: Apps and documents are open, if they were open before Sleep.

- **Shut Down:** This option exits Windows 11 and saves power by turning the computer off. In exiting Windows 11, Shut Down closes any apps that are currently running.

- **Restart:** Temporarily shuts down Windows 11 and turns it on again. Use Restart when Windows 11 asks you to or when Windows 11 is misbehaving.

TIP

You can also shut down your computer by using the Start button. Move the pointer over the Start button and right-click. A pop-up menu appears. Select Shut Down or Sign Out on the pop-up menu, and then select an option (Sleep, Shut Down, or Restart).

4. Choose Shut Down to turn off the computer.

TIP

On most computers, pressing the power switch also shuts down the computer, though you should use the Shut Down option in Windows 11 rather than press the power switch button. On a laptop, closing the lid may shut down the laptop or put it in sleep mode. However, if you're going to store your computer in a bag or travel with it, shut it down first to make sure that it doesn't overheat inside the bag.

Start Again on the Lock Screen

1. Turn on your computer. Every time you turn on your computer, the Lock screen appears. As shown in **Figure 1-10**, the Lock screen displays the time, day, and date along with a background image. (You discover how to change this image in Chapter 3.)

2. Dismiss the Lock screen with one of these methods:

   - **Mouse:** Click anywhere, roll the wheel toward you, or drag the entire screen up.

   - **Touchscreen:** Drag the entire screen up.

   - **Keyboard:** Press any key.

3. If you don't use a password or Windows Hello to sign in, wait briefly for the Start screen to appear. If you use a password, enter it with a physical or touch keyboard. Then press Enter or select the arrow next to the password box to display the Windows desktop screen.

FIGURE 1-10

TIP

When you take a long break from your PC, it automatically goes to sleep. Windows 11 puts your computer to sleep to save battery life. To decide for yourself how much time passes before your computer goes to sleep, select the Search box on the taskbar and type **lock screen** in the Search box. Choose Lock Screen Settings in the search results. On the Personalization > Lock Screen window, scroll down the screen to the Screen Timeout and select it. You come to the Power & Sleep screen. Choose a setting from the Sleep menu. For example, choose 15 minutes to put your computer to sleep after 15 minutes of inactivity.

Connect Your Phone to Windows 11

Windows 11 can connect with and sync with your phone. This capability means that if someone calls or texts you while you're using Windows 11, you can answer that phone call or text using your computer. You don't even have to reach for your phone to do so!

Windows 11 uses a built-in app called Phone Link to connect with your phone. Here's how you set it up:

1. In the Search box on the taskbar, type **phone link**.

2. Select Phone Link from the search results.

3. On the Phone Link screen, choose Android or iPhone (depending on what kind of phone you use). The app then asks you to sign into your Microsoft account.

4. The next screen gives you a QR code to scan with your phone's camera (shown in **Figure 1-11**). To scan the code, just open your camera app and point your camera at the code (don't take a picture of it). Then follow the instructions on your phone to complete the Phone Link setup.

FIGURE 1-11

TIP

Phone Link uses Bluetooth wireless technology to connect to your phone. Bluetooth must be enabled on your phone for the connection to work. See your phone's documentation for more information.

IN THIS CHAPTER

» **Opening, closing, and switching between apps**

» **Introducing the app bar**

» **Tweaking app settings**

» **Having fun with widgets**

» **Chatting with Copilot AI**

Chapter **2**

Using the Start Screen, Apps, Widgets, and Copilot

The Windows 11 *Start screen* appears when you select the Start button on the taskbar or you press the ⌘ key. It provides access to just about everything you do with Windows 11.

The Start screen is home to numerous programs, or apps (short for applications). An *app* performs a function or displays information. For example, the Weather app offers weather reports (surprise!), and the Maps app helps you map a route between two places. Apps can be simple or complex.

Apps appear on the Start screen as icons. An *icon* displays the app's name and symbol for the app. An open app typically covers the screen, hiding other apps that are open. However, some apps can be displayed side-by-side with a function called *snap.*

Windows 11 also provides easy access to a group of mini apps called *widgets.* Widgets are graphical apps that give you fast at-a-glance information about news, sports, weather, stocks, and so forth. You choose what widgets you want to see and quickly view them using the Widgets icon on the taskbar.

In this chapter, you open, close, and use some of the apps that come with Windows 11. You also switch between apps and the Start screen, and switch directly between two apps. You find out how to search for apps not shown on the Start screen. You discover how to organize the Start screen by rearranging and pinning apps. You also explore how to add and remove widgets.

Finally, you take a look at Copilot, the Artificial Intelligence (AI) digital assistant in Windows 11, and have some fun chatting with it.

See Chapter 10 for information on getting new apps from the Microsoft Store.

TIP

Although some steps are specific to one app, most of the steps you follow in this chapter can be repeated in any app.

Open Windows 11 Apps

1. Select the Start button taskbar, as shown in **Figure 2-1**. Selecting this button opens the Start screen, also shown in **Figure 2-1**.

   You can also open the Start screen by pressing the ⌘ key.

2. On the Start screen, you see a group of apps. These apps are *pinned* to the Start Screen, meaning that they always appear (you can change what's pinned, and you find out how in "Pin and Unpin Apps on the Start Screen," later this chapter). Click the All Apps button to see an alphabetical listing of all apps available on your computer. Select All Apps and then locate the Weather app and select it. The Weather app opens to the Forecast screen, as shown in **Figure 2-2**. It shows the current temperature and weather forecast for your default location. You see some basic toolbar options on the left. Select the Show Options button (refer to **Figure 2-2**). As do most apps, Weather has a Show Options button in the upper-left corner. Select this button to expand the app bar and see the names of options on the app bar. Select the button again to collapse options on the app bar.

Start screen　　　　　　　　　　　　**All apps**

Start button

FIGURE 2-1

TIP

The first time you open the Weather app, a Welcome screen appears. It asks whether you want to show temperatures in Fahrenheit or Celsius and what your location is. By location, the Weather app wants to know where you live, or, if you're a vagabond, where you spend the majority of your time. Choose Detect My Location or enter a city or town name in the Search box, and from the menu that appears as you type, select the name of the town or city that you call home. You can always change these settings by selecting the Settings button in the app bar and choosing options on the Settings screen. (See the section "Change App Settings," later in this chapter.)

App bar

Show Options

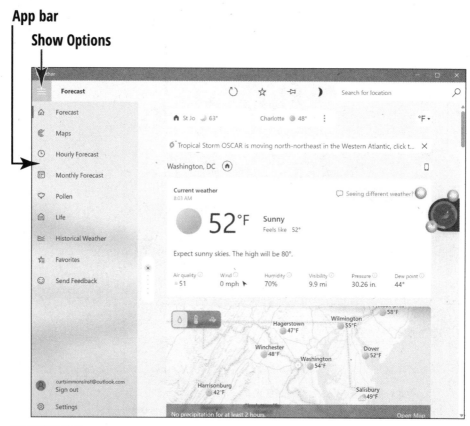

FIGURE 2-2

3. Switch back to the Start screen using one of these methods:
   - Tap or click the Start button.
   - Press the ⌘ key.

TIP

Focus on the method you think is easiest. However, keep in mind that alternative methods of controlling your computer are always available.

4. Switch back to the Weather app (it's now behind the Start screen) by selecting its title bar with the mouse or your finger. The Weather app reappears and the Start screen disappears.

5. Switch back to the Start screen.

6. Select the Microsoft Edge icon (it's probably pinned in your app list on the Start screen). The Edge browser opens to your home page, as shown in **Figure 2-3**.

FIGURE 2-3

TIP

If the Edge icon doesn't appear on your Start screen, select the All Apps button and locate it in the alphabetical list.

TIP

Edge is a *browser*, which is an internet application for exploring the web. Chapter 6 covers Edge in detail.

7. Scroll downward to see all that is on the web page you are visiting. Use these techniques to scroll:

   - **Mouse:** Drag the scroll box on the right side of the screen up or down. If your mouse has a wheel, you can also turn the mouse wheel to scroll.

   - **Touchscreen:** Swipe the screen up or down.

8. Close Edge and the Weather app. Use one of these methods:

   - **Mouse:** Click the Close button (the X) in the upper-right corner of the app's window.

   - **Touchscreen:** Tap the Close button (the X) in the upper-right corner of the app's window.

   - **Keyboard:** Press Alt+F4.

TIP

Chapter 5 explains how you can open a second desktop on the screen and in so doing keep some of your open apps on one screen and some on another. When you're running many apps, opening a second desktop is a great way to be able to switch quickly from one app to another.

TIP

Open apps appear as icons on the taskbar, but when you close an app, its icon disappears from the taskbar. Some icons appear permanently on the taskbar. For example, the File Explorer icon is always on the taskbar regardless of whether File Explorer is running. Chapter 5 explains how you can pin your favorite apps to the taskbar. Pinning an app to the taskbar places an icon there so that you can open an app quickly.

TIP

Press Alt+Tab and continue to hold down the Alt key after you press Tab. A window showing thumbnails of all open apps appears onscreen. While holding down the Alt key, press the left- or right-arrow key to move between the open apps to select one; then release the Alt key. The Weather app appears onscreen. Pressing Alt+Tab is yet another way to switch between open applications.

TIP

Chapter 5 demonstrates techniques for moving windows onscreen, changing the size of windows, and snapping windows to the side of the screen.

TIP

To close an app that is frozen (an app that is unresponsive), press Ctrl+Shift+Esc. The Task Manager opens. It lists all apps that are currently running. Select the app you want to close and then select the End Task button.

Use the App Bar

1. From the Start screen, open the Weather app if it isn't already open.

2. The *app bar* contains functions specific to the current app. Display the app bar by selecting the Show Options button. (Refer to **Figure 2-2**.)

TIP

Depending on the app, the app bar may appear across the top of the screen, the left side of the screen, or in both locations.

3. In the Weather app, the app bar leads you to different functions. Select Maps, for example, to see a weather map of the area where you live, shown in **Figure 2-4**.

4. Display the app bar in Weather again. Then select Historical Weather. A screen appears showing you weather trends over the past 12 months.

5. Display the app bar again and take notice of the Home icon. Wherever you travel in an app, you can return to the app *home screen* by selecting this icon.

TIP

In most apps, you can select the Back button (a left-pointing arrow) to return to the previous screen you viewed. The Back button is found in the upper-left corner of most screens.

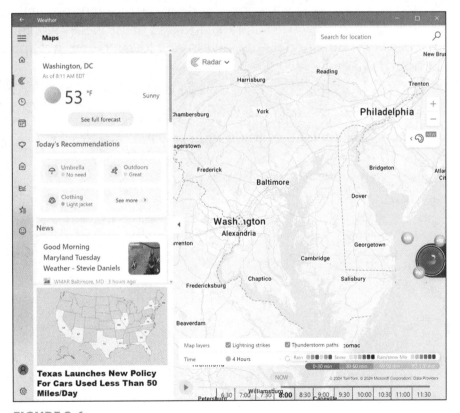

FIGURE 2-4

Add a Location in Weather

1. From the Start screen, open the Weather app if it isn't already open. With the Weather app on the screen, select the Show Options button to expand the app bar and see the option names (refer to **Figure 2-2**).

2. Select the Favorites button on the app bar. The Favorites screen appears, as shown in **Figure 2-5**. Your screen will show a different Launch Location.

3. Select the Add to Favorites icon, which looks like a plus sign in a square. The Add to Favorites screen appears.

4. Type a location name, such as a city, in the box under Add to Favorites, as shown in **Figure 2-6**. As you type, matching location names appear below the box. If you see the location you want, select that name to add an icon for that location to the Places screen. No need to click the Add button, unless your location does not appear automatically.

You can add other locations by repeating Steps 3 and 4.

TIP

5. Select the icon for the location you added. The Weather app displays full information for the location you selected.

FIGURE 2-5

TIP

You can switch among multiple locations by using the Favorites button on the app bar.

TIP

Select Favorites in the app bar to see a screen with weather locations you chose (refer to **Figure 2-6**). From there, you can select a weather location to get reports and predictions about weather in a different city or place.

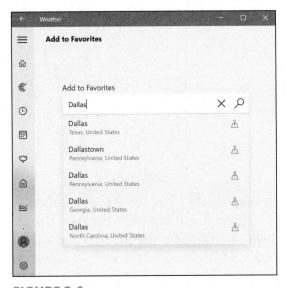

FIGURE 2-6

Change App Settings

1. On the Start screen, select the Weather icon if the Weather app isn't open already.

2. In the Weather app, select the Settings button on the app bar. The Settings screen appears, as shown in **Figure 2-7**. Settings is the bottommost option on the app bar. If you have trouble locating it, select the Show Options button, the topmost button on the app bar, to see the buttons on the app bar.

FIGURE 2-7

TIP

It may be hard to remember whether you need the Settings panel or the app bar to do something. In general, functions on the app bar are used more frequently than those on the Settings panel. When in doubt, guess — that's how discoveries are made.

3. Choose whether to show air temperatures in Fahrenheit or Celsius.

4. Choose a Launch Location option. The Always Detect My Location option tells the Weather app to note by way of your internet connection where you are currently and give the weather report for that place. Select Default Location and enter the name of the place where you live if you want to receive weather forecasts for that place.

TIP

Select Privacy Statement in the Settings window if you're interested in how Microsoft collects data about you when you use Weather and other apps made by Microsoft. You see a page clotted with legalese and other obfuscations.

Search for an App

1. Open the Start screen. A Search box appears at the top, as shown in **Figure 2-8**. If you select the Search box to type a search, the screen automatically changes to the Search screen, shown in **Figure 2-9**. More easily, you can just select the Search box on the taskbar to search for an app (or anything else!).

2. In the Search box, type **calc** (the first four letters of the word *calculator*). The Search window shows you the results of your search, as shown in **Figure 2-10**. You can search for just about anything from the Search box.

Search box

FIGURE 2-8

FIGURE 2-9

FIGURE 2-10

TIP

Select a filter option at the top of the Search panel (see **Figure 2-11**) to redirect your search. For example, select Apps to search only for apps, Documents to search for files on your computer, select Web to search the web, and so forth. **Figure 2-11** shows you an example of filtering a calculator search to only the web. This example shows internet results for various online calculator tools and websites.

3. Type **ulator** to finish typing the word *calculator*. The Search panel lists only items with the complete word *calculator* in them, including the Calculator app.

4. Select the Calculator app to open it on the desktop, as shown in **Figure 2-12**. To perform a calculation, select the buttons on the screen or use a keyboard.

5. Close the Calculator app by selecting the Close button at the top right of the app.

Search filter options

FIGURE 2-11

FIGURE 2-12

Pin and Unpin Apps on the Start Screen

1. Open the Start screen. Your computer has numerous apps already pinned to the Start Screen for easy and fast access. However, you may not want some of these default apps pinned, and you may want some apps pinned that are not. You can easily change the pinned apps any time. Select the All Apps button and locate the Calculator button in the alphabetical list.

2. Display the Calculator app's context menu using one of these methods:

   - **Mouse:** Right-click Calculator icon.

   - **Touchscreen:** Touch and hold the Calculator icon until the context menu appears, and then release your finger.

3. On the context menu, choose Pin to Start, shown in **Figure 2-13**.

4. Select the Back button to return to the Start screen's main window. The Calculator app is now pinned to your Start screen and appears in the Pinned group.

5. To unpin the Calculator app from the Start screen, display its context menu again and choose Unpin from Start.

FIGURE 2-13

TIP

When you unpin an app from the Start screen, it simply removes the app's icon from the Pinned group. The app is still safe and sound on your computer. You can pin and unpin any apps you want at any time so that you see only pinned apps that you frequently use.

Arrange Apps on the Start Screen

1. You can rearrange icons on the Start screen by dragging them to different places. On the Start screen, drag the Calculator icon to a different location. As you move the icon, other icons move out of the way, like a game of Dodge Icon.

2. To drag an app, select the app's icon with your left mouse key and hold down the key. Then just drag the icon to a new location in your Pinned apps. If you're using a touchscreen, just press and hold the app's icon with your finger and drag.

3. Continue this process until you have organized the app icons in a way that is helpful to you. For example, you may organize the apps in a list starting with the most frequently used to the least frequently used, or you can even place them in alphabetical order. You can rearrange the pinned apps at any time by repeating these steps.

Do you have one app you want first in the list? Just display the app icon's context menu and choose Move to Front.

TIP

Uninstall an App

1. You can download apps from the Microsoft Store (see Chapter 10), but a time may come when you want to uninstall an app. For example, say you download a game but don't find it particularly fun. You no longer want the app on your computer. Good news! You can easily uninstall it. Open the Start screen and select the All Apps button.

2. Locate the app you want to uninstall in the alphabetical list.

3. Display the app icon's context menu using one of these methods:

   • **Mouse:** Right-click the app's icon.

   • **Touchscreen:** Touch and hold the app's icon until the context menu appears, and then release your finger.

4. Choose Uninstall on the context menu, shown in **Figure 2-14**. A dialog box appears telling you the app will be removed. Select the Uninstall button on the box. The app is then removed from your computer.

After you uninstall an app from your computer, it's gone. The only way to get it back is to redownload it from the Microsoft Store.

TIP

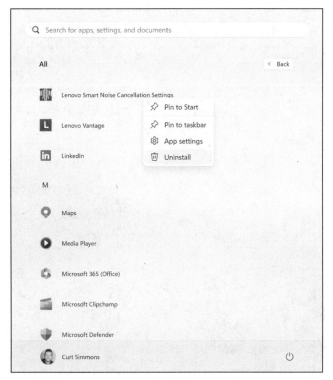

FIGURE 2-14

Use the Widgets Panel

1. On the left side of the taskbar, select the Widgets icon to open the Widgets panel, shown in **Figure 2-15**. The Widgets icon may look like the weather or some other information, such as news or stocks. This icon varies depending on your computer's default settings.

2. The Widgets panel has four tabs at the top left of the panel:

   - **Home:** Home is the default panel location. The home screen displays a section of news stories and even ads, called channels. Windows shows you channels that you may be interested in seeing (but don't be surprised if you're not!). On the right side, a vertical panel of widgets appears that you can add to or remove. (You see default widgets based on your computer's setup.). See **Figure 2-16**.

Widgets icon

FIGURE 2-15

News stories

Home

Following

Watch

Play

Your widgets

Add widgets

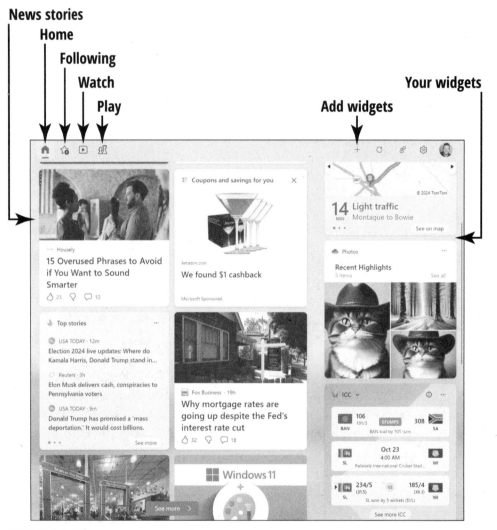

FIGURE 2-16

- **Following:** Click Following to see any channels you may have chosen to follow. To add a channel, just click the Add Channel button and then select a channel in the list to follow. For example, you can choose to follow the Stocks channel or the Pets channel.

On the home page, if you see a channel you want to follow, just point to the channel and select the See More button that appears; then select Follow.

Following channels helps Windows know what you're interested in seeing. Windows then uses this information to show you other channels that are similar.

- **Watch:** This option changes the news stories to videos. Windows 11 picks videos that it thinks you may want to watch.

- **Play:** This option changes the default news stories to a bunch of game options you may want to play if you enjoy games.

3. Aside from following channels, you can also add widgets. To add a new widget, select the Add Widgets button (see **Figure 2-16**). In the Pin Widgets window, select the widget you want to add in the left panel and then click the Pin button on the right (see **Figure 2-17**). For example, try adding the Traffic widget by selecting Traffic in the left panel and clicking Pin. You can add multiple widgets at the same time. When you're done, close the window by clicking the Close button. The Traffic widget (or any others you added) now appear on the left side of the home screen.

FIGURE 2-17

Windows 11 gives you a set of widgets to choose from, but the Microsoft Store has more. Select the Add Widgets button on the main Widgets panel (refer to **Figure 2-16**); then, on the Pin Widgets window, select Find More Widgets at the bottom left of the window. Some of the additional widgets are free and some aren't, but the Microsoft Store will give you the details and pricing of each widget.

Unpin a Widget

1. Open the Widgets panel by clicking the Widgets icon on the taskbar.

2. To unpin a widget, select the More Options button on the upper-right corner of the widget. On the menu that appears, choose Unpin Widget, shown in **Figure 2-18**.

When you unpin a widget, it's simply removed from your Widgets panel. It's not removed from your computer. You can select the Add Widgets button anytime and simply pin the widget again.

FIGURE 2-18

Customize a Widget

1. Open the Widgets panel by clicking the Widgets icon on the taskbar.

2. You can change the size of widget. Select the More Options menu located in the upper-right corner of the widget. You can choose from Small, Medium, or Large. In **Figure 2-19**, all the widgets are set to Small.

3. To change the size of the widget, just select the size you want from the More Options menu. Widgets do not have to be the same size. For example, in **Figure 2-20**, the Markets widget is set to Large and the Traffic widget is set to Medium

TIP

Larger widgets typically display more information. Consider making your most important widgets larger and keep the less important widgets smaller.

FIGURE 2-19

FIGURE 2-20

4. You can also customize the data you see on each widget. The customization options vary based on the widget and what the widget does. For example, add the Traffic widget to your widgets (if it's not already added). Then select More Options and choose Customize Widget, as shown in **Figure 2-21**.

5. On the customization window, you can specify a location, such as a city and state, as shown in **Figure 2-22**, or you can choose to detect your location. The second option is helpful if you travel frequently; that way, the widget is always accurate wherever you're located. Make your selection and choose Save.

Remember, widgets are designed to give you quick information. The idea is that you open the Widgets panel and immediately see information that is important to you. Keep this thought in mind as you choose, organize, and customize your widgets as well as channels.

FIGURE 2-21

FIGURE 2-22

Chatting with Copilot AI

1. Select the Copilot icon on the taskbar to open the Copilot app. Copilot is an Artificial Intelligence (AI) digital assistant. You can ask Copilot questions and Copilot will use the internet to find answers for you. Copilot is a fun and easy way to gather information quickly.

TIP

If you have a Copilot + PC, your computer has an optimized processor for Copilot, and you'll see a Copilot key on your keyboard. Just press the Copilot key to open Copilot.

TIP

When you start Copilot for the first time, you may need to sign in with your Microsoft account and select a Get Started button. Just follow any prompts you see.

2. At the bottom of the Copilot window, you can type a message to start chatting with Copilot. You can also select the microphone icon to talk instead of typing. You computer must have a microphone for this feature to work. Start with something simple. Type or say **show me a strawberry cake recipe**. Copilot replies and gives you a recipe to try, as shown in **Figure 2-23**.

3. Continue the conversation. Type or say **show me a photo of this recipe**, or you can ask other specific questions about the recipe.

FIGURE 2-23

TIP

Copilot uses the internet to locate images for you. In some cases, images may not be available.

4. Try something a bit more complex. Type or say **what are the top vacation destinations in the United States and which is most expensive**. Copilot replies with a response. Notice the link at the bottom of the response, as shown in **Figure 2-24**. This link tells you where Copilot got the information. You can click the link and visit the web page to read all the information from the article.

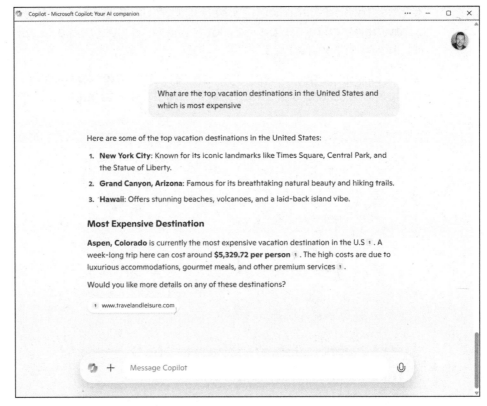

FIGURE 2-24

5. You can try even more complex conversations. Type or say **I have ten thousand dollars to invest for five years. I want to get the maximum return with a medium risk tolerance. What are my best options?** Copilot replies with a response. The response picks up on the concepts of risk and tolerance to form an answer. Also, notice

the links at the bottom of the answer where you can get more information. You can also continue the conversation by asking a follow-up question. Type or say **tell me more about index funds**. Copilot replies with a response. You can continue chatting this way for as long as you like!

Copilot can provide good and succinct information, but it's not perfect. For important questions (such as investments, health, and others), always fact-check the information you get. Also, as a side note, Copilot doesn't like to talk about religion, politics, and other controversial topics. Copilot may give you some basic information but avoids opinion-oriented questions for many topics.

6. Copilot is great for answering questions, but you can also have some fun. Try typing or saying one or all of these options:

   - **Write a song about Paris.**
   - **Tell me a joke about a dog.**
   - **Show me a photo of the Grand Canyon.**
   - **Tell me why a cat would make a good leader.**
   - **All humans should go to bed by 8 p.m. Reply with an argument as if you're a parrot.**
   - **If an alien could see our planet, what would the alien think about our skyscrapers?**

7. Copilot can also create drawings and images for you. Type or say **draw an image of a red bird**. After Copilot creates the image, you can download and save it. Just click the Download button next to the image, shown in **Figure 2-25**. You can also reply to the image and make modifications. For example, try statements like **give the bird a hat**, **make the bird scary**, **make the bird drive a car**. The sky is the limit! Select Close on the Copilot window when you're done.

When you start Copilot, you can access previous conversations. Just click the View History icon to the left of the Copilot message box.

Do you want to print or share a Copilot conversation? Select the Settings and More button on the Copilot toolbar (it looks like three dots) and then point to More Tools.

Download image

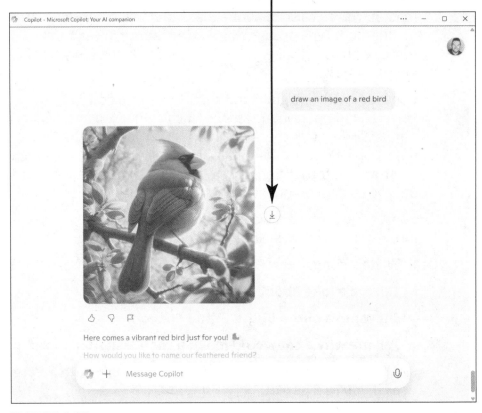

draw an image of a red bird

Here comes a vibrant red bird just for you! 🖐

How would you like to name our feathered friend?

FIGURE 2-25

Chapter **3**

Adjusting Windows 11 Settings

O ut of the box, Windows 11 is showy and colorful. If you don't like that look, however, you can change the photos and colors you see on the screen. Adjusting Windows 11 settings can also make Windows 11 easier and more fun to use. When you're ready, you can dive in and make Windows 11 yours.

In this chapter, you personalize the Lock screen. You see this screen many times a day, so it should please you. You also choose a picture to identify your account on the Start menu. This chapter also explains how to make your screen easier to see and enable features such as Narrator, which reads aloud content from the screen. Finally, you discover how to customize the Start menu and decide which notifications pop up in the lower-right corner of your screen.

Many people leave Windows 11 largely as they found it. Some love to tweak, tinker, and tune. How far you go in personalizing Windows 11 is up to you — it's your computer, after all.

See Chapter 4 for information on changing passwords and other User settings.

TIP

Access the Settings Screen

1. Select the Search box on the taskbar and search for Settings.

2. Choose the Settings app in the search results, as shown in **Figure 3-1**.

Turn to Chapter 2 if you need help opening an app on the Start menu.

TIP

3. The Settings screen appears, as shown in **Figure 3-2**. The Settings screen is the starting point for changing the settings here, there, and everywhere on your computer.

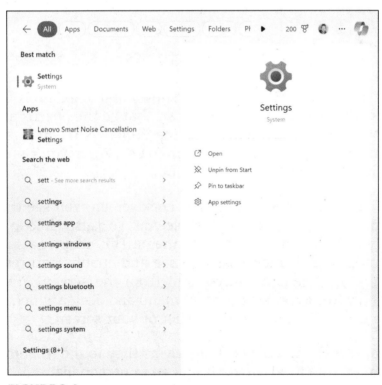

FIGURE 3-1

4. One at a time, select each icon in the Settings screen, starting with System, to see the options available. Select the Back button (the left-pointing arrow, located in the upper-left corner of the screen) to return to the Settings screen.

5. On the Settings screen, enter the word **printer** in the Search box (located at the top of the screen; refer to **Figure 3-2**). As soon as you enter the word, the Settings screen shows you a list of settings that pertain to printers. You can select a setting on the list to open the dialog box where the setting is located.

FIGURE 3-2

Windows 11 offers many different settings. Locating them can be a chore. Often the easiest way to find a setting is to enter its name in the Search box on the Settings screen. Also, you can search for any setting using the Search box on the taskbar.

TIP

Personalize the Lock Screen

1. On the Settings screen, select Personalization.

2. On the Personalization screen, scroll down and select the Lock Screen option on the right side. The Lock Screen Preview screen opens, as shown in **Figure 3-3**. On the Personalize Your Lock Screen drop-down menu, you see three options, as shown in **Figure 3-3**.

   - **Windows Spotlight:** This option displays an image that Microsoft chooses. The image will change frequently, giving you a nice variety of beautiful photos (typically nature shots).

   - **Picture:** This option allows you to choose a photo from your collection that is currently on your PC (such as in your Pictures folder).

   - **Slideshow:** This option allows you to rotate through a collection of photos that will appear on the Lock screen as a slideshow. If you choose this option, all the images need to be in the same folder on your computer.

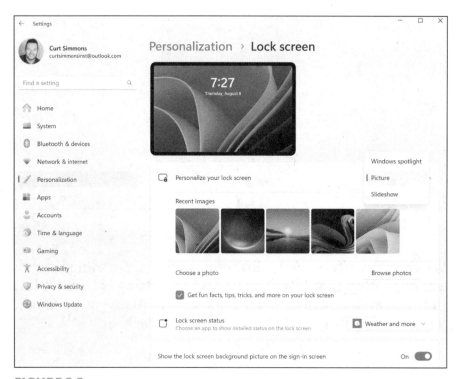

FIGURE 3-3

Choose Picture to select one of your images.

TIP

The Lock screen is the first screen you see when you start Windows 11.

3. You can select from recent images that appear after you select the Picture option. You can also click the Browse Photos button to search for a specific photo, as shown in **Figure 3-4**.

TIP

You can use the Browse button to select one of your own photos from the Pictures folder. See Chapter 15 for information on adding photos to this folder and its subfolders.

4. After you select a picture, it will display on the Lock screen. You repeat these steps at any time to choose a different picture, or you can choose Slideshow or Windows Spotlight.

Choose Picture

Choose a recent image

Browse for a photo

FIGURE 3-4

TIP

You can lock your computer anytime by pressing ⌘+L. Make sure you know your password or that your computer is configured with a Windows Hello login before locking your computer. See Chapter 1 for details about starting again from the lock screen.

Choose an Account Picture

1. On the Settings screen, select Accounts on the left panel. See "Access the Settings Screen," earlier in this chapter, if you need help opening the Settings screen. Scroll down and select Your Info in the Account Settings section. Your current Account picture appears on the right, as shown in **Figure 3-5**. (If you haven't selected a picture yet, your picture may just be an outline.)

FIGURE 3-5

TIP

Your account picture appears on the password screen and the Start screen as well as other locations in Windows 11 where your account is noted.

2. To choose one of your photos, select the Browse Files button. The contents of your Pictures folder appears in the Open dialog box. From here, you can select the File Explorer navigation pane to access any folder on your computer or select a subfolder to open. When you find the picture you want, select it and then select the Choose Picture button. Or select Cancel to return to the previous screen without changing your account picture.

TIP

See Chapter 11 for information about adding photos to your Pictures folder.

3. If you have a built-in or attached camera (called a *webcam*), select the Open Camera button to take a photo. The Camera app opens with a preview of what your camera sees, as shown in **Figure 3-6**. See Chapter 11 for information on taking pictures with a webcam.

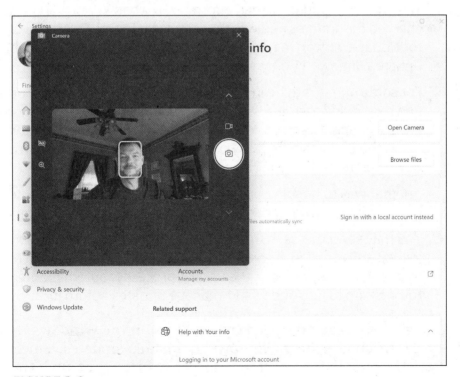

FIGURE 3-6

4. Return to the Start screen to see your new account picture. To return to the Start screen, click or tap the Start button or press ⌘ on your keyboard.

The easiest way to access the Accounts screen and change your account picture is through the Search box on the taskbar. Type **Your Info** and the option to go to Your Account Info screen directly appears in the search results. Click that search result, and voilà! The Accounts screen appears, with Your Info selected.

Check for Important Updates

1. To check for updates to Windows 11, select Windows Update on the left panel of the Settings screen. See "Access the Settings Screen," earlier in this chapter, if you need help getting to the PC Settings screen. The Windows Update screen, shown in **Figure 3-7**, appears.

2. The Windows Update screen informs you when Windows 11 last checked for updates and whether any were found. Select the Check for Updates button to find out whether any updates are available and update Windows 11 on your computer.

3. For some updates to be installed, your computer has to shut down and restart. In cases like this, you see the Restart Now button on the Windows Update screen. You can select the Restart Now button to install the updates right away or just wait until the next time you shut down and restart on your own to install the updates.

Another way to handle updates is to simply leave your computer on overnight. Windows 11 performs the update as you sleep.

4. You may see a message that one or more updates will be downloaded and installed automatically. You do not have to do anything to install these updates — the update process is automatic. Return to the desktop to let Windows 11 manage updates automatically.

You can select the Advanced Options link on the Windows Update screen to choose how Windows 11 installs updates. Select the View Update History button and get a history of updates that Windows 11 has made to your computer.

FIGURE 3-7

TIP

Installing an update seldom takes more than a few minutes. You can use your system during the update process.

TIP

For information on other updates and maintaining Windows 11, see Chapter 13.

Make Windows 11 Easier to Use

1. On the Settings screen, select Accessibility. (See "Access the Settings Screen," earlier in this chapter, for help.) The Accessibility screen, shown in **Figure 3-8**, appears. This screen offers many settings to make your computer, mouse, and monitor easier to use. These settings are organized into three categories: Vision, Hearing, and Interaction. (You need to scroll down the window to see all the settings.)

FIGURE 3-8

TIP

Here's a quick way to open the Ease of Access screen: Press ⌘+U (for *usability*).

2. Under Vision, choose the Text Size settings (refer to **Figure 3-8**). These settings make the screen easier to view and read by making the text larger or smaller.

3. Also under Vision, choose the Mouse Pointer and Touch settings to change the size and color of the mouse pointer. As shown in **Figure 3-9**, Windows 11 offers mouse pointers of different sizes and colors. Choose the combination that tickles your fancy.

4. Also under Vision, choose Text Cursor settings to change the color and thickness of the text cursor. The *text cursor* is the vertical line that appears onscreen to show you where text will appear when you begin to type.

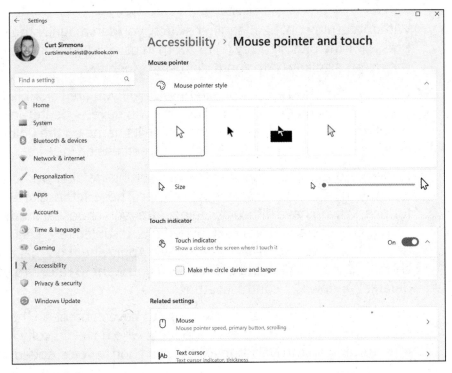

FIGURE 3-9

5. Again under Vision, choose Magnifier settings to enlarge what is on your computer screen. These settings are for people who have difficulty seeing. When Magnifier is turned on, the screen automatically magnifies to the current Zoom level. You can adjust the Zoom level by pressing ⌘ + the plus sign (+) or ⌘ + the minus sign (–), as shown in **Figure 3-10**.

FIGURE 3-10

TIP

Without turning on the Magnifier switch, you can magnify the screen. Press ⌘ + the plus sign key (+) to zoom in using Magnifier. Press ⌘ + the minus sign key (–) to zoom out using Magnifier.

6. Under Vision, choose a Color Filters setting if you are color blind. If you know which type of color blindness you have — deuteranopia, protanopia, tritanopia — you can choose its name on the Color Filters menu to make seeing items onscreen easier.

7. Under Vision, choose Contrast Themes settings to alter the screen in a way that may make seeing text easier. These settings are also for people who have difficulty seeing. After you choose a theme, you can choose a color for text, hyperlinks, disabled text, selected text, button text, and backgrounds. Click Apply after you make your choices. Choose None and click Apply if you want to return to the default Windows 11 contrast settings.

8. Under Vision, choose Narrator settings to have content on the screen read aloud. These settings are for people who have difficulty reading. After turning on the Narrator switch, you choose voice, speed, and pitch settings to determine what the narrator's voice sounds like.

9. Under Hearing, choose Audio Settings to increase the default volume and control whether you hear stereo or mono sound on your computer. If you have poor-quality speakers, turning the Mono Audio option to On can improve the sound.

10. Also under Hearing, choose Captions settings to control how subtitles appear in audio and video presentations. Choose Font settings to describe what you want the text in the captions to look like. Choose Background and Window settings to describe what the box where the captions appear looks like. The Preview box shows what your choices mean in real terms.

11. Under Interaction, choose Speech settings to dictate text instead of typing it and control your computer and device with voice commands.

12. Also under Interaction, choose Keyboard settings to type without using a physical keyboard. This onscreen keyboard uses the layout of a conventional keyboard. However, most people find that the standard Windows 11 virtual keyboard is more flexible. See Chapter 1 for information on the virtual keyboard layouts.

13. Again under Interaction, choose Mouse settings if for some strange reason you want to control the mouse with the keys on the numeric keypad.

14. Finally, under Interaction, choose Eye control. This feature allows you to use an eye-tracking device to control the screen by using your eyes. You have to have a tracking device for this to work. You can select the link on this screen to get more information about setting up and using an eye-tracking device.

Customize the Start Menu

1. On the Settings screen, select Personalization. See "Access the Settings Screen," earlier in this chapter, if you need help opening the Settings screen.

2. On the Personalization screen, select Start. The Personalization > Start screen opens, as shown in **Figure 3-11**. This screen offers a few ways to customize the Start screen. First, you can choose a Layout option. The default is a mix of pins and recommendations, but you can choose to see More Pins or More Recommendations instead. Just select the button of the layout you want.

3. You can turn the following items on or off (refer to **Figure 3-11**):

   - **Show Recently Added Apps:** Places the names of apps you recently acquired on the Start menu.

   - **Show Most Used Apps:** Places the names of programs you use most often on the Start menu. The names of these programs appear under the Recommended heading.

   - **Show Recommended Files in Start, Recent Files in File Explorer, and Items in Jump Lists:** Allows you to quickly open folders, files, and windows from the Start menu, taskbar, and File Explorer screen. When you move the pointer over an app or program on the Start menu, an arrow appears; select the arrow to see a menu of items you can open. When you move the pointer over an icon on the taskbar, thumbnail windows appear so that you can choose which window to open. In File Explorer, the items are listed in the Quick Access section of the navigation pane.

- **Folders:** Allows you to place specific folders on the Start menu. These folders appear next to the Power button after you place them there. For example, you might want to add your Documents or Pictures folder to the Start menu for fast and easy access.

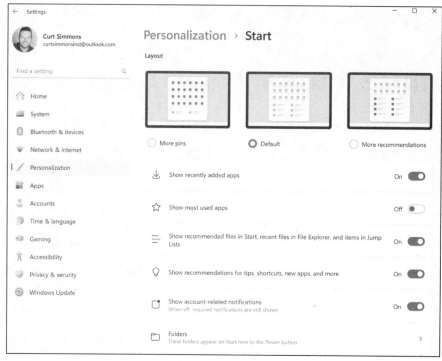

FIGURE 3-11

Handle Notifications

1. *Notifications* are the sometimes pesky little message boxes that appear in the lower-right corner of the screen when you least expect them. You can decide for yourself whether notifications appear and which notifications you want to see. On the Settings screen, select System. See "Access the Settings Screen," earlier in this chapter, if you need help opening the Settings screen.

2. Select Notifications to see the screen shown in **Figure 3-12**.

3. Under Notifications in the Notifications from Apps and Other Senders list, turn options on or off to tell Windows whether you want notifications to appear on your screen.

4. Select the Close button (the *X*) to close the Settings window.

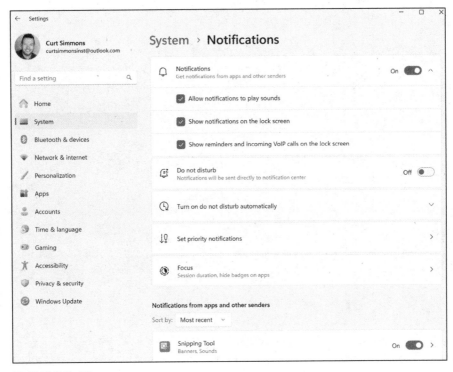

FIGURE 3-12

Chapter **4**

Working with User Accounts

Windows 11 seeks an internet connection automatically from the moment you start it. More often than not, you connect to the internet using a wireless or *Wi-Fi* connection. For this reason, if you start a laptop or tablet in a coffee shop or library, you may see a notification that one or more network connections are available. That's convenient.

A computer without an internet connection is an island, if not a paperweight. Connecting to a network, however, opens a door to your computer — and malefactors try to push through that door to access your computer. Windows 11 has a *firewall* that monitors and restricts traffic in and out. Don't be afraid of connecting to the internet, but be aware of the risks and be careful to connect to a network that seems trustworthy. In Chapter 1, you create a local user account. You need a Microsoft account to take full advantage of Windows 11 features such as the Microsoft Store for apps (see Chapter 10), OneDrive for online storage (see Chapter 16), and synchronized settings between computers. In this chapter, you create a Microsoft account and choose a secure method for logging in to your account. You also discover how to switch to Airplane mode, create a local account, and switch from a local account to a Microsoft account. To control access to your computer, you find out how to use a password to unlock your computer.

If other people use your computer, you may want to create more than one local account. When each person who uses your computer has a separate account, you can keep data, apps, and settings tidy and private. I recommend having only one administrator account for each computer.

Even if you're the only one using your computer, you may want more than one account. For example, if you create a local account, you can experiment with the new account — changing the look and function of Windows 11 — without affecting your first account.

Many of the steps in this chapter involve entering text, such as your name. If you don't have a physical keyboard, use the virtual keyboard, which is covered in Chapter 1.

Connect to the Internet

1. On the Windows desktop, look to the Network icon to see whether your computer is connected to the internet. This icon is located to the left of the time and date readings in the lower-right corner of the screen on the taskbar, as shown in **Figure 4-1**.

Select or choose options by moving the mouse pointer and left-clicking or by tapping a touchscreen with your finger.

2. Select the Network icon. A network panel (see **Figure 4-2**) appears on the right side of your screen and shows what network you are connected to. Select the Wi-Fi button to see available networks, as shown in **Figure 4-3**.

If you see *Not connected* and *No connections available,* you may be out of luck. Check your computer documentation to see whether your PC has wireless capability and whether you need to turn on a mechanical switch.

Network Connection icon

FIGURE 4-1

Network Connection

FIGURE 4-2

FIGURE 4-3

TIP

If your computer is near a router and you don't have wireless capability, you may be able to connect your PC and the router using an Ethernet cable, which is thicker than a phone line and has wider connection points (RJ45 connectors).

3. Select a network connection. Note that not all displayed connections are accessible or desirable.

TIP

If you're not sure that you can trust a connection, you may want to forgo a connection — better safe than sorry. (Unsafe wireless connections can be used to eavesdrop on your activities, though that scenario is rare.) However, if an available connection sports the name of the establishment you're in or near, such as a restaurant or a coffee shop, the connection may be safe. The same is true of connections at libraries, airports, and many other public spaces.

4. After you select a connection, the selected icon expands and displays the Connect Automatically check box, as shown in **Figure 4-4**. If you trust the connection and may want to use it again, select the check box. Otherwise, deselect the check box. To continue, select the Connect button.

FIGURE 4-4

5. You may be prompted to enter a password (also called a network security key), which limits access to those who know the password. See **Figure 4-5**. The password protects that network and its users. If you're using a hotel's connection, you can obtain the password from the front desk. If you don't know the password, select Cancel. Otherwise, enter the password (dots appear as you type) and select Next.

TIP

If the connection is public and open, you may not be prompted for a password. Open connections are common in libraries, coffee shops, and other places many people come and go.

FIGURE 4-5

6. If you entered the correct password or none was required, you may see this message: *Do you want to turn on sharing between PCs and connect to devices on this network?* The term *sharing* refers to allowing computers access to your files or to a device, such as a printer. You should share at home but never in a public location. Choose one of the following:

- **No:** This option prevents you from connecting directly with other computers and protects your computer from networks in public places. You'll still have internet access.

- **Yes:** This option enables you to share documents and devices between your computers on a home or office network.

TIP

If you're not sure about which option to choose, go with No.

7. When a Wi-Fi connection is established, the word *Connected* appears next to the network name in the Networks panel, as shown in **Figure 4-6**. The connection name and signal strength appear as well. The connection strength (but not the name) appears near the time and date in the notification area in the lower-right corner of the screen (see **Figure 4-1**).

FIGURE 4-6

TIP

If you selected the Connect Automatically check box (in Step 4), the connection will be used anytime it is available. If you move your computer to another location out of range of this network (usually a few hundred yards), you will have to repeat these steps to connect to another network.

Disconnect (or Switch to Airplane Mode)

1. When you shut down your computer or move your computer far enough away from the connection, your computer disconnects from the internet automatically. Suppose you want to disconnect on your own? To disconnect your computer from the internet, select the network icon on the taskbar to display the network panel again (refer to **Figure 4-2**).

2. To turn off Wi-Fi, just select the Wi-Fi button (the button changes from blue to white). To reconnect, select the Wi-Fi button again (the button changes back to blue). (If you disconnect your computer, reconnect before continuing to Step 3.)

3. For safety's sake, airlines don't want passengers to send or receive wireless data signals while the airplane is in flight; these signals can interfere with the airplane's communications systems. This is why the captain gives the order to "turn off all electronic devices." Rather than turn off your computer, however, you can switch to Airplane mode. To do so, open the network panel and select the Airplane Mode button. This button is located in the group of buttons at the top of the network panel.

4. In Airplane mode, an airplane icon appears to the left of the time and date readings in the lower-right corner of the screen, as shown in **Figure 4-7**. Your computer doesn't send wireless data signals in Airplane mode. To switch out of Airplane mode and reconnect to the internet, select the airplane icon to display the network panel. Then select the Airplane Mode button (refer to **Figure 4-2**).

Airplane mode

FIGURE 4-7

TIP

Switching to Airplane mode is much more convenient than turning off your computer's network connection and turning it back on again. It takes but a second or two.

Create a New Microsoft Account

1. On the Start screen, select your picture on the bottom left side of the screen. In the pop-up menu that appears, choose My Microsoft account, as shown in **Figure 4-8**. The Settings app opens to the Accounts screen, as shown in **Figure 4-9**. If your account information

appears with the words *Local Account* under your name, you are signed in with a local account. If you don't see Local Account, you already have a Microsoft account and don't need to follow these steps.

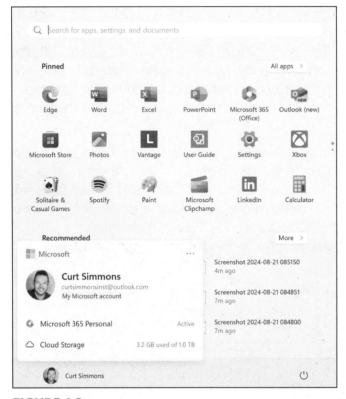

FIGURE 4-8

2. Select the Sign In with a Microsoft account Instead link. The Sign In screen appears. To create a new account, select the Create One! link.

3. On the Create Account screen, create the account with an email address or a phone number. Messages about your Microsoft account will be sent to the email address or phone number you enter.

   • **Email address:** Type the email address you want to use for this account in the Email Address box and select Next.

   • **Phone Number:** Select the Use a Phone Number Instead link. Then enter your phone number and select Next.

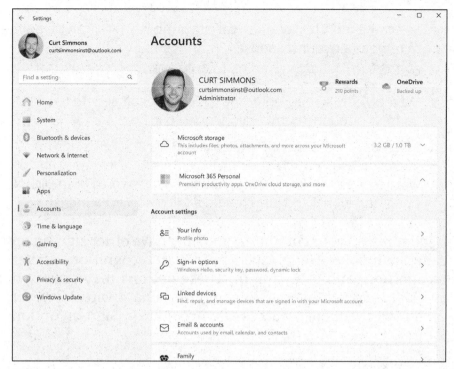

FIGURE 4-9

4. In the Create a Password box, type a password. Dots appear instead of what you type. Use at least eight characters, including at least two uppercase letters, two lowercase letters, two numbers, or two symbols. No spaces are allowed.

TIP

Your password should be easy enough for you to remember and type, but not easy for someone else to guess. Don't use the names of any family members (including pets). A good password can be difficult to create, so try this trick: Think of a memorable phrase or lyric. Next, use the first letter from each word, capitalizing some of those letters. Then substitute some letters with numbers (for example, 3 for the letter *E* or the number 0 for the letter *O*). Don't put your password on a sticky note near your screen.

5. Enter your first and last name, then select Next.

6. In the What's Your Birth Date? screen, enter your country or region if it is not already selected.

7. Select the month, day, and year of your birth. (You can lie, but be sure to remember your response.)

8. Review your entries and select the Next button.

9. On the Verify screen, enter the code Microsoft sent to the email address or phone number you entered in Step 3.

10. Select the Next button. The Sign In to This Device Using Your Microsoft account screen appears. Enter the user name and password to your local account, if you had a password. Then click Next. Congratulations! You just created a Microsoft account.

Depending on your computer, you may have other sign-in options called Windows Hello, such as facial recognition, fingerprint recognition, and PIN sign-in. These options may or may not be available depending on your computer's hardware. However, you can check them out by accessing Accounts ⇨ Sign-in options.

Create a Local Account

1. "Local account" is Microsoft's name for your ability to start your computer without signing in to Microsoft. Before you create or sign in with a local account, save your work. Then enter **settings** in the search box on the taskbar. Choose Settings in the search results. Select Accounts in the Settings app. On the right side of the screen, choose Your Info, and under Account Settings choose Sign in with a Local Account Instead (shown in **Figure 4-10**).

You can't download and install apps from the Microsoft Store without signing in with a Microsoft account. Nor can you upload files to OneDrive. So why have a local account? If you're concerned about privacy and security, or if you don't want Microsoft to peer over your shoulder and track your every move when you use your computer, consider creating a local account. You can always switch to your Microsoft account when you want to install apps from the Microsoft Store, use OneDrive, or use Skype (see "Switch from a Local to an Existing Microsoft Account," later in this chapter).

FIGURE 4-10

TIP

To create a local account for someone else to use your computer, see "Create a Local Account for Someone in Your Household," later in this chapter.

2. You see the Switch to a Local Account screen, shown in **Figure 4-11**. Select the Skip This Step button and select Next on the following screen.

3. Enter the password of your Microsoft account on the Making Sure It's You screen, shown in **Figure 4-11**, and select OK.

4. In the next screen, enter a user name, a password (twice), and a word or two to jar your memory if you forget your password; then select Next.

TIP

Passwords are case sensitive. In other words, your computer recognizes uppercase letters and lowercase letters when you create and enter a password. Remember which letters in your password are upper- and lowercase.

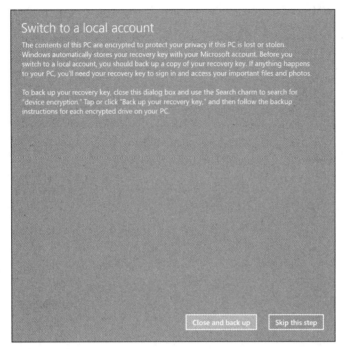

Switch to a local account

The contents of this PC are encrypted to protect your privacy if this PC is lost or stolen. Windows automatically stores your recovery key with your Microsoft account. Before you switch to a local account, you should back up a copy of your recovery key. If anything happens to your PC, you'll need your recovery key to sign in and access your important files and photos.

To back up your recovery key, close this dialog box and use the Search charm to search for "device encryption." Tap or click "Back up your recovery key," and then follow the backup instructions for each encrypted drive on your PC.

Close and back up   Skip this step

FIGURE 4-11

TIP

If you want to sign in to your local account without having to enter a password, leave the Password, Reenter Password, and Password Hint text boxes blank. Later in this chapter, the sections "Create or Change a Password for a Local Account" and "Change an Account Type" explain the ins and outs of local account passwords.

5. Select the Sign Out and Finish button. Your Microsoft account closes, Windows restarts, and you see the Windows 11 screen.

6. Enter the password you created in Step 3. When you start your computer, Windows 11 assumes that you want to sign in with the account you were using when you last shut down your computer. If you shut down when signed in with your local account, you are asked to provide the password for your local account the next time you start your computer.

Switch from a Local to an Existing Microsoft Account

1. Follow these steps to sign in with your Microsoft account when you are currently signed in with your local account. Return to the Settings app and choose Accounts (refer to **Figure 4-8**). The Accounts screen opens. Your account information appears with *Local Account* under your name.

TIP If you don't have a Microsoft account already, see "Create a New Microsoft Account," earlier in this chapter.

TIP If you don't see *Local Account* under your user account name, you're already signed in with your Microsoft account.

2. Select the Sign In with a Microsoft account Instead link. Type the email address or phone number of your Microsoft account and select the Next button. Note that you must be connected to the internet to sign in with a Microsoft account.

3. Enter the password of your Microsoft account and select the Sign In button.

4. In the Current Windows Password text box, enter the password of your local account and select the Next button. The Accounts screen opens, where you see the user name and email address of your Microsoft account.

Create a Local Account for Someone in Your Household

1. Consider creating a local account for each person who uses your computer. A local account is more than just a way to sign in. Each local account preserves the user's settings and internet browsing history. When you set up a local account, Windows 11 creates separate folders called Documents, Pictures, Videos, and Music for the account holder. Only the account holder can open and edit files in these special folders. To create a local account, return to the Settings app and choose Accounts. (refer to **Figure 4-8**). The Settings app opens to the Accounts screen.

To create a local account, you must be your computer's administrator. To see whether you're the administrator, look for the word *Administrator* below your name on the Your Info page of the Settings screen.

2. Scroll down the Accounts pane to see options for both Family and Other Users. If you select Family, you can choose to find out more about Family settings, where you can enable some specific features pertaining to family safety, activity reporting, content filters, and so forth. You can also add a family member by choosing Add Someone to Your Family Group and Allow Them to Sign In on This Device (see **Figure 4-12**). If you want to create an account for someone who is not family, you can choose the Other Users option on the Accounts screen. This option opens an Add Account option (shown in **Figure 4-13**). Select the button here to add account. The How Will This Person Sign In screen appears.

FIGURE 4-12

FIGURE 4-13

3. At the bottom of the How Will This Person Sign In screen, select the link called I Don't Have This Person's Sign-In Information (shown in **Figure 4-14**).

TIP

If you know you want a Microsoft account instead of a local account, jump to "Create a New Microsoft account" or "Switch from a Local to an Existing Microsoft account," earlier in this chapter.

4. On the next screen, select Add a User without a Microsoft account.

5. On the next screen (it's called Create a User for This PC), enter the user name in the first box, as shown in **Figure 4-15**. Use the person's first name, last name, first and last name, initials, or nickname — something easy to remember and type.

TIP

You are not required to use a password with a local account, which makes signing in easy. However, without a password, anyone can use the computer and access information that you might want to protect.

6. In the Password box, enter a password (or skip to Step 9 if you don't care to create a password for your account). A dot will appear for each character you type.

FIGURE 4-14

FIGURE 4-15

TIP

For suggestions on creating a good password, see the tip in Step 4 in the section, "Create a New Microsoft Account," earlier in this chapter.

7. In the Reenter Password box, type the same password exactly.

8. Choose a security question and type the answer in the text box. If you forgot your password, you will be able to recover it by answering a security question correctly.

9. After completing all the available boxes, choose the Next button. In the Accounts screen, the new user name appears under Other Users, as shown in **Figure 4-16**.

10. Return to the Start screen and select your user name. Notice that you can choose Switch User in the drop-down menu to switch between accounts.

11. A screen appears with the new user name. If you used a password on the new user account, type that password in the box and select the onscreen right arrow or press Enter. If you didn't use a password, select the Sign In button.

FIGURE 4-16

TIP

The first time you sign in as a new user, you have to wait a moment while apps are installed for the new user. Soon the generic Start screen appears. (Any settings you changed in your account do not transfer to other accounts.)

TIP

When you start a computer for which you've created more than one user account, the users' names appear in the lower-left corner of the Windows 11 screen. To tell Windows which user to sign in with, select a user name on the Windows 11 screen before signing in.

Create or Change a Password for a Local Account

1. If necessary, sign in to the local account that needs a password. Open the Settings app and select Accounts. Scroll down the page and choose Sign-in Options, and then choose Password. Here, you can add or change the password. (see to **Figure 4-17**).

2. On the Create a Password screen, enter a password in the New Password box.

TIP

If you're changing an existing password, you need to enter the current password first.

For a local account, the password can be any length. See Step 4 in the "Create a New Microsoft Account" section for suggestions about creating a good password.

3. In the Reenter Password box, enter the password again.

4. Enter a hint to remind yourself — and no one else — about your password. And whatever you do, don't include the password in the hint.

5. Select Finish. If any error messages appear, correct the entries and select Next again.

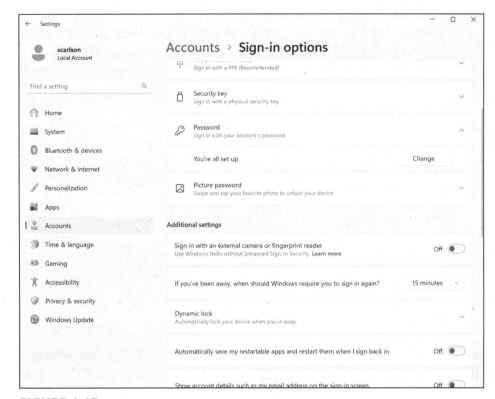

FIGURE 4-17

Change an Account Type

1. Access the Settings app and choose Accounts. On the right side of the window, select the account you want to change. When you create a new family or other user account, that account is considered a standard user. You can't use that account to make administrative changes to the computer. However, you can change a standard account to an administrator account if you need to.

TIP

Use caution with administrator accounts. An administrator can make system-wide changes to Windows, including adding or removing other accounts. Typically, you want one administrator (and that probably shouldn't include your pre-teen grandchildren!). The administrator can change any settings, delete programs and apps, and even add new programs and apps.

2. To change an account type, choose the Change Account Type button. You see the default as Standard User. You can use the drop-down menu to change the account type to Administrator, and then click OK (see **Figure 4-18**).

Change account type

Change account type

scarlson
Local Account

Account type

Administrator

Standard User

OK   Cancel

FIGURE 4-18

Delete a Local Account

1. Before you delete a local account, make sure that the user of that account is signed out. Moreover, you must be signed in to a Microsoft account to delete a local account.

2. Open the Settings app and choose Accounts. Locate the local account you want to delete under the Family or Other Users categories.

3. Select the account you want to delete and then select the Remove button next to Account and Data, as shown in **Figure 4-19**.

4. In the Delete Account and Data window, select the Delete Account and Data button.

FIGURE 4-19

TIP

Take heed of the onscreen warning. Deleting a user account removes the user's data, including all documents, music, and other files. If you're not sure which option is best, choose Cancel.

Chapter **5**

Getting Comfortable with the Desktop

The *desktop* is Grand Central Station as far as Windows 11 is concerned. Sure, you can open applications from the Start screen (Chapter 2 explains how), but with a few simple modifications, you can open applications from the desktop as well. When you're running more than one application, you can go to the desktop and quickly switch from one application to another. In fact, in Windows 11, you can create a second "virtual" desktop for one set of open applications (applications that pertain to leisure, say), and when the boss isn't looking, you can switch to the second desktop to play games or chat with friends.

One key feature of the desktop is the *taskbar*, a strip along the bottom of the screen that shows icons for desktop programs. You can use the taskbar to run and switch among desktop programs.

In this chapter, you get acquainted with the desktop, the taskbar, and apps. You change the date, time, and time zone, as needed. You resize and reposition windowed apps, and discover how to "add a desktop" for a second set of open applications. You select a background for the desktop and make some desktop apps more convenient to use by pinning them to the taskbar. Finally, you work with the Task Manager, which lets you end any app that is misbehaving.

The desktop originated when using *the* mouse was the most common method for selecting objects (touchscreens were nonexistent). Therefore, on the desktop, a few tasks are easier to do with the mouse than with touch or a keyboard.

TIP

This chapter is an introduction to the desktop. See Part 4 to dive a little deeper into desktop *functions*, such as organizing documents.

TIP

Check Out the Desktop

1. Go to the desktop (if you aren't already there) by using one of these techniques:

   - Press ⌘+D.

   - Right-click the Windows button and choose Desktop on the pop-up menu that appears.

2. Your desktop has a picture in the background. Examine your desktop for *icons* — small pictures that represent either programs, which perform functions, or documents, such as letters and photos. You select an icon to run a program or open a document. The Windows 11 desktop displays an icon for the Recycle Bin, where deleted documents go. The Recycle Bin may be the only icon on your desktop, or you may see others. See Chapter 15 for information on using the Recycle Bin.

3. The area at the bottom of the screen is the *taskbar,* shown in **Figure 5-1**. From left to right, the taskbar offers these features:

   - **Widgets:** This far-left taskbar icon may appear as the weather or even news, but it's actually a collection of mini-programs and features called widgets. See Chapter 2 for details.

TIP

   - **Start button:** Selecting this button opens the Start screen. (Click or tap the button a second time to close the Start screen.)

FIGURE 5-1

- **Search button:** You can select Search to open the Search screen and enter a search term here to look for Windows settings, applications, files on your computer, and information on the internet.

- **Virtual Desktop:** Select this button to create an additional virtual desktops (see "Open a Second Desktop," later in this chapter, for more information).

- **Icons:** Some icons appear on the taskbar automatically. Very likely, your taskbar has icons for Copilot, File Explorer, and Edge. You can select these icons to open those programs. When you open any application, Windows 11 places its icon on the taskbar.

- **System tray:** The *system tray* displays icons for programs that run automatically when your computer starts. The date and time are to the right of the icon tray. On the right side of the icon tray is the Notification icon.

You can use the taskbar to switch among programs by selecting the icon for the program you want to use.

4. Select an icon on the taskbar to open the associated program. (Refer to **Figure 5-1** if you aren't sure where the taskbar is located.)

TIP
You select items on the desktop or in the taskbar by clicking with the mouse or tapping the touchscreen. To some extent, you can use the Tab and arrow keys, but that's an awkward method.

TIP
If you have a touchscreen, note the taskbar icon for the virtual keyboard. See Chapter 1 for information about using the keyboard.

5. Right-click over an icon or tap and hold until a small box appears, and then release. A *context menu* appears with options specific to the icon you selected, as shown in **Figure 5-2**. Select anywhere else on the desktop to dismiss this menu. Repeat this action on a few different areas of the screen to see how the context menu changes.

Installed apps

Mobility Center

Power Options

Event Viewer

System

Device Manager

Network Connections

Disk Management

Computer Management

Terminal

Terminal (Admin)

Task Manager

Settings

File Explorer

Search

Run

Shut down or sign out   >

Desktop

FIGURE 5-2

Change the Date or Time

1. Select the date and time displayed on the taskbar. A calendar pops up, as shown in **Figure 5-3**.

2. If the date or time is incorrect for your location, select the Search box on the taskbar and then search for Date and Time settings. Select the option in the search results. You can also right-click the date and time in the system tray and select Adjust Date & Time. Either way, the Settings screen opens. Select Time & Language. You see the Date & Time window, shown in **Figure 5-4**.

FIGURE 5-3

3. Windows 11 determines the correct time and date from the internet, and your computer should show the right time and date, but if it doesn't, turn off the Set Time Automatically option and select the Change button. You see the Change Date and Time screen (see **Figure 5-5**). Select the correct date and time on this screen. Change the time by using the little triangles that point up (later) or down (earlier) or by entering the specific hours and minutes. Select Change to keep your change or Cancel to ignore your change.

4. Back in the Date and Time window, select your Time Zone from the drop-down list, if necessary. Turn the Adjust for Daylight Saving Time option on or off as appropriate.

5. Note the toggle button for Adjust for Daylight Saving Time Automatically. If you live in an area where daylight saving time is in effect, keep this button turned on so that your computer will automatically adjust for daylight saving time.

Turn off automatic time   **Adjust your time zone**

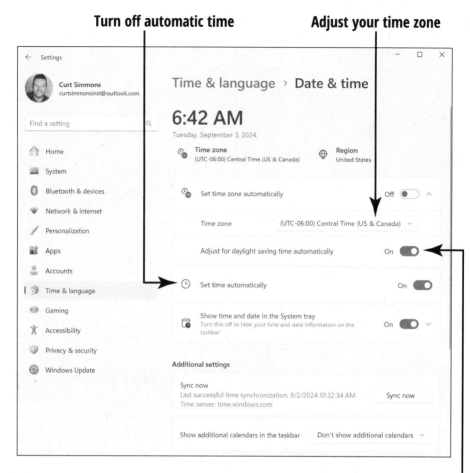

FIGURE 5-4

Change date and time

Date

September   3   2024

Time

6   47   AM

Change   Cancel

FIGURE 5-5

Explore the Parts of a Window

1. On the taskbar, select the File Explorer icon (it looks like a folder). File Explorer opens, as shown in **Figure 5-6**.

TIP

File Explorer enables you to view your computer storage, such as hard *drives*, and folders, which you use to organize your documents. See Chapter 15 for information on using File Explorer.

2. Explore the example window in **Figure 5-6**, starting at the top left:

   • **Title bar/title tab:** The *title bar* is the area along the top of the window, which may or may not have an actual title. The *title tab* lists the name of the file or folder that is currently open.

TIP

The title tab of the window in **Figure 5-6** is Home, which is the location File Explorer is focused on when you open File Explorer.

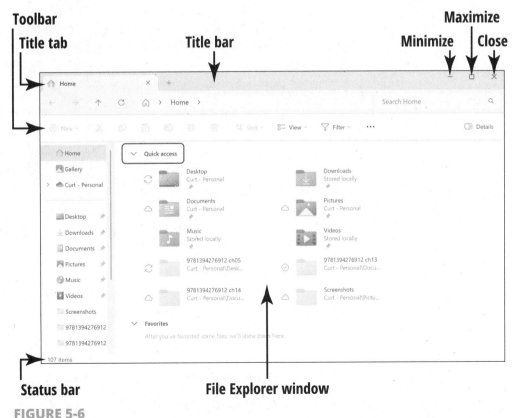

FIGURE 5-6

- **Toolbar:** The toolbar gives you access to common tools, such as Cut, Copy, Paste, Sort, View, and others.

- **Minimize:** The *Minimize button,* located in the upper-right corner of the window, shrinks or hides the window's contents. The program that the window contains is still running and open, but the window is out of sight. You'll still see the program's icon on the taskbar. Select the Minimize button when you want to ignore a particular window but aren't actually done with it. To restore the window, select its icon on the taskbar.

- **Maximize/Restore:** The *Maximize button* (the button with a single square in the upper-right corner of the window) fills the screen with the contents of the window. Select the Maximize button to hide the desktop and other open windows, to concentrate on one window, and to see as much of the window's contents as you can. The *Restore button* (the button with two squares in the upper-right corner) is the name of the button that appears after you select the Maximize button; it replaces the Maximize button. Select the Restore button to return the window to its previous size, which is between maximized and minimized. (Press ⌘+up-arrow key to maximize, and ⌘+down-arrow key to restore or minimize.)

- **Close:** The *Close button* is the button with the X in the upper-right corner of the window. Select the Close button when you are done with the window. Close is also called Quit and Exit. (Press Alt+F4 to close the current window or the desktop itself. This keyboard shortcut works for Windows 11 apps, as well.)

- **Window Contents:** The bulk of the window contains the program or document you're using. File Explorer displays locations on the left and objects in that location on the right.

- **Status bar:** Along the bottom edge of the window, some programs display information about the window or its contents in a single-line *status bar.* File Explorer lists how many files are in the currently open folder and how many files (if any) have been selected.

Scan the edges of windows. Often, important information and functions are pushed to these edges around the main content pane.

3. Select the Close button (the X) to close File Explorer.

See Chapter 2 for *information* on finding other desktop programs, such as the Calculator.

TIP

Resize a Window

1. To resize a window, open File Explorer by selecting the folder icon in the taskbar. (Refer to **Figure 5-1**.)

2. If the window is maximized (fills the screen), select the Restore button to make the window smaller.

3. Use one of these methods to resize the window:

   • **Mouse:** Move the mouse pointer to the right edge of the window until the pointer changes to a double-headed arrow, called the *resize pointer.* Click and drag the edge of the window, using the resize pointer. (To drag, click, and hold down the mouse button while you move the mouse.)

   • **Touchscreen:** Drag the right edge of the window.

   Drag left to shrink the window and right to expand it.

TIP

4. Resize the window's width and height at the same time by dragging a corner of the window. If you want a challenge, try resizing the top-right corner without accidentally selecting the Close button.

5. Resize the window's width *or* height by dragging any of the four sides.

   You may want to resize a window to show only what you need to see, nothing more. Practice resizing from any side or corner.

TIP

6. Leave the window open as you go on to the next task.

Arrange Some Windows

1. On the desktop, select and open the Recycle Bin by double-clicking or double-tapping its icon. The Recycle Bin contains deleted files and folders. It appears in another File Explorer window. See **Figure 5-7**.

Double-click by clicking the left mouse button twice, without a pause. Double-tap by tapping twice in quick succession.

2. If File Explorer isn't still open from the preceding section, open it by selecting the folder icon on the taskbar. You now see two overlapping windows on the desktop (refer to **Figure 5-7**), one titled *This PC* and the other titled *Recycle Bin*.

The window in front of the others is called the *active* window. All other windows are *inactive.* Selecting anywhere in an inactive window makes it active and moves it to the front of the others.

3. Drag the Recycle Bin title bar (avoiding the buttons on the left and right ends) to move that window a little.

4. Drag the This PC title bar (again, avoiding the buttons on both ends). The This PC window moves in front of the Recycle Bin as you move it. Move both windows so that you can see a little of each (refer to **Figure 5-7**).

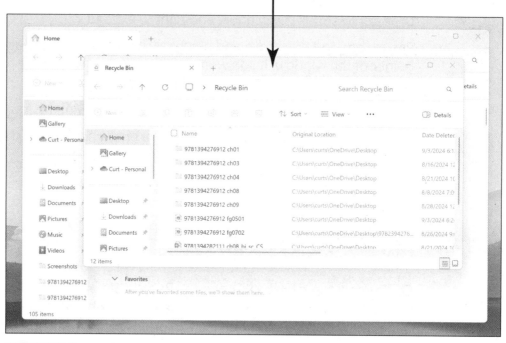

FIGURE 5-7

5. Practice moving both windows. Arranging windows helps you see and do more than one thing at a time. Use the techniques from the preceding section, "Resize a Window," to see as much as you can of both windows at one time.

If you can't see the title bar of the window you want to move, move the other window to uncover the hidden title bar.

6. Leave both windows open for the following task.

Use Snap Layouts

1. With the File Explorer window and Recycle Bin open, also open the Edge browser and the Windows Store (both are available as icons on the taskbar).

2. Now you have four different windows open on your desktop. That's a lot of windows to manage. What if you're trying to work with all of them at the same time? You would have to toggle back and forth between those windows, which would be time consuming and confusing. Windows 11 provides an easy and fun way to work with several windows at the same time on the desktop, called Snap Layouts. Point your mouse to the Maximize button on one of the windows (it doesn't matter which one), and you see a pop-up menu appear, as shown in **Figure 5-8**.

3. Each snap layout group represents an area of the desktop that you can snap the selected window to. For example, choose the left block in the first snap group and then choose the right block in the first snap group for a second window. This snaps both windows in place so that you can easily work with them at the same time, as shown in **Figure 5-9**.

4. What if you have four open windows? In that case, just choose the four-window snap layout and snap each open window to the desired location. For example in **Figure 5-10**, File Explorer, Recycle Bin, Edge, and the Windows Store are snapped into a four-grid layout.

5. In the snap view, you can work with each window without minimizing the others. To move a window out of a snap view, just drag its title bar or select the Maximize button. Then you can move the window around, resize, or close it as you normally would.

FIGURE 5-8

FIGURE 5-9

FIGURE 5-10

TIP

You can maximize a single window by dragging it to the top edge of the screen. Dragging a window to the top is the equivalent of selecting the Maximize button (see the section "Explore the Parts of a Window," earlier in this chapter).

Open a Second Desktop

1. If File Explorer and Recycle Bin aren't open on your desktop (because you didn't follow the previous exercise in this chapter), open those programs now.

2. Select the Virtual Desktop button on the taskbar. After you select the Virtual Desktop button, a thumbnail version of an open desktop appears, and you see an option to select New Desktop, as shown in **Figure 5-11**.

3. Select New Desktop. You see a brand-new, pristine desktop, labeled Desktop 2, as shown in **Figure 5-12**. Congratulations; you are now in Desktop 2. Create a second (or third or fourth) desktop when you want to keep the first desktop from getting crowded with too many

applications or to better organize your work. For example, if you're using applications for your work and using other applications for leisure purposes, put the work applications on one desktop and the leisure applications on another. This will help you find the application you want to work with.

4. While you are on Desktop 2, open the Photos app. Having just one application on the desktop makes working with that application a little easier.

5. Move the pointer or your finger onto the Desktop 2 tile, and when the Close button appears, click or tap the Close button to close Desktop 2. The Photos app that you opened on Desktop 2 now appears on Desktop 1, the only open desktop. When you close a desktop, all its open applications move to the desktop that is still open.

FIGURE 5-11

FIGURE 5-12

Choose a Desktop Background

1. Select the Search box on the taskbar and search for Settings. Choose the Settings app in the search results.

2. Select Personalization. Then, in the Personalization window, select Background. The Background screen, shown in **Figure 5-13**, is the place to go to choose a background for the Windows desktop.

   TIP

   You can use the Personalization window to customize many aspects of the desktop. The more time you spend on the desktop, the more worthwhile this personalization may be.

3. In the Personalization window, select Picture on the Background menu (see **Figure 5-13**).

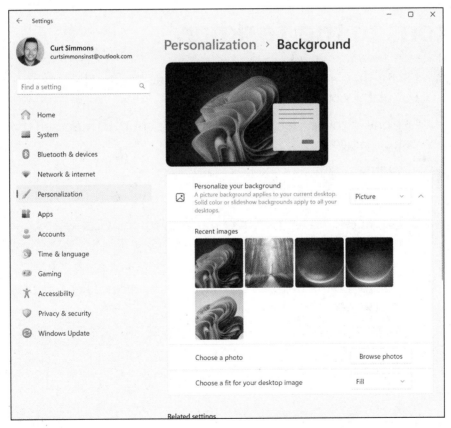

FIGURE 5-13

4. Select any photo to make that photo the desktop background. The background changes immediately. To see the entire desktop, minimize the Settings window. Restore the Settings window by selecting its icon on the taskbar or by repeating the preceding steps.

To use a photo of your own as the desktop background, select the Browse button and choose a photo in the Open dialog box.

Note that on the Personalization window, you can choose Themes and apply a different theme to your Windows 11 PC. Doing so will affect the desktop photo, colors, and possibly even sounds. You can also download free themes from the Microsoft Store to make Windows 11 even more personalized. See Chapter 10 to find out more about the Microsoft Store.

Pin Icons to the Taskbar

1. On the Start screen, select the All Apps button and locate the Calculator icon, as shown in **Figure 5-14**.

2. Use one of these methods to display the shortcut menu on the Calculator icon:

    - **Mouse:** Right-click the Calculator icon.

    - **Touchscreen:** Swipe the Calculator icon down or up slightly.

3. Select More on the shortcut menu. A submenu with more options appears (see **Figure 5-15**).

4. Select Pin to Taskbar on the submenu. Doing so places the icon for Calculator on the desktop taskbar for easy access. The Calculator icon appears on the taskbar.

Press ⌘+D to go directly to the desktop at any time.

FIGURE 5-14

5. Repeat Steps 1 and 3 and then select Unpin from Taskbar.

TIP

A fast way to remove an icon from the taskbar is to right-click it and choose Unpin from Taskbar on the shortcut menu.

6. Switch to the desktop. The Calculator icon is gone.

TIP

Pinned icons have a killer feature: *jumplists,* which are short menus of tasks and documents specific to the pinned app. To see the jumplist of a pinned app, right-click its icon on the taskbar or tap and hold on the icon until a small box appears. Try that with the File Explorer icon on the taskbar. Not all desktop apps have jumplists.

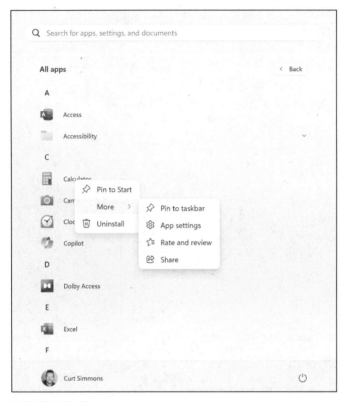

FIGURE 5-15

Stop Apps with the Task Manager

1. Select the Search icon on the taskbar and search for Task Manager. Select Task Manager from the search results.

2. The Task Manager lists any running apps — both desktop apps and Windows 11 apps. Select an app, also referred to as a *task*. Note that the End Task button is now available, as shown in **Figure 5-16**. You don't have to end this task, but you could. Any of the tasks in the Task Manager window can be ended without consequences except possible data loss if you haven't saved it.

TIP

Be careful about ending an app used to create something (for example, a word-processing app) because you could lose data you haven't saved before ending the task. Use the Task Manager to end tasks that you can't end otherwise, such as a frozen or locked app or one that seems to slow down everything.

3. Close the Task Manager.

Selected app   End task

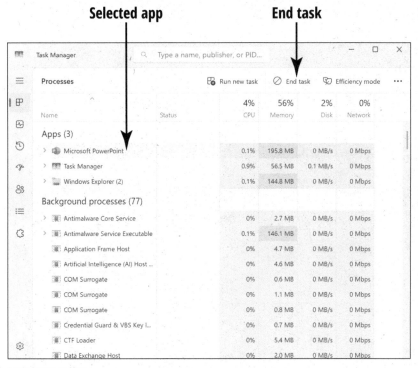

FIGURE 5-16

2

Windows 11 and the Web

Chapter **6**

Finding What You Need on the Web

The World Wide Web — or, simply, the web — provides quick access to information and entertainment worldwide. One part library, one part marketplace, and one part soapbox, the web makes everything equidistant. From down the block to halfway around the world — even out into space — everything is a few clicks or taps away. News, shopping, and the electronic equivalent of the town square await you.

You explore the web using a *web browser*, a program designed to make browsing the web easy, enjoyable, and safe. In this chapter, I show how you can use the Edge browser to step beyond your computer into the global village.

You browse *web pages*, which are published by governments, businesses, and individuals — anyone can create web pages. Each web page may consist of a few words or thousands of words and pictures. A web page is part of a larger collection called a *website*, which consists of a group of related web pages published on a topic by an organization or individual. Companies and individuals create websites to organize their related pages.

Pages and sites on the web have some common characteristics:

» **Unique addresses**, which are formally called *URLs* (URL stands for Uniform Resource Locator, in case you're ever on *Jeopardy!*).

» **Connecting links** that move you from page to page when you select them. These *links* (also called *hypertext links* or *hyperlinks*) often appear underlined and blue. Pictures and other graphic images can also be links to other pages. You can tell when a picture or image is a link by moving the pointer over it. The pointer changes from an arrow to a hand when it is over a hyperlink picture or image. Exploring the web using links is easier than typing URLs.

In this chapter, you use Edge to browse the web. To get the most out of browsing, you juggle multiple sites simultaneously and find out how to bookmark your favorite websites. You also find out how to search for almost anything and make use of some nice features in Edge, including Copilot AI. Finally, this chapter shows how to view web pages without seeing pesky advertisements.

TIP

Edge is by no means the only browser — it's just Microsoft's browser. You can also download and try other browsers if you like, namely Mozilla Firefox (www.mozilla.org) and Google Chrome (www.google.com/chrome/browser). With that said, note that Edge does everything you need, so you don't need to download anything else.

Browse the Web with Edge

1. Open Edge by selecting its icon on the taskbar. Edge opens to the *start page,* as shown in **Figure 6-1**. This page presents websites and news stories that Microsoft thinks are of interest to you based on your browsing history. If you haven't used Edge yet or haven't used it very often, you don't have a browsing history to speak of, and the websites and news stories you see here probably look quite tepid.

TIP

When you start Edge, you may see an error message if you're not connected to the internet. If so, see Chapter 4 for information on connecting. See "Bookmark and Revisit Your Favorite Websites," later in this chapter, for instructions about choosing a home page.

2. Note the *address bar* at the top of the Edge screen (refer to **Figure 6-1**). In the address bar, type `www.dummies.com`. As you type, search suggestions appear in a drop-down menu. Either select `www.dummies.com` in the search suggestions or press Enter. The web page for the Dummies Press appears, as shown in **Figure 6-2**.

TIP

If you have trouble finding the address bar, try clicking with the mouse or tapping with your finger near the top of the screen, to the right of the four buttons (Back, Forward, Refresh, and Home). This will make the address bar appear.

Address bar

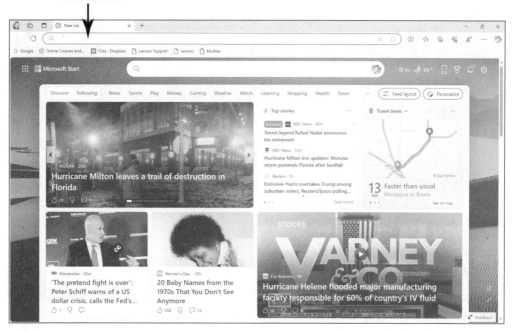

FIGURE 6-1

3. Select a link on the page with a click or a tap. Where are the links? Just about everywhere. When you move the pointer over a link, it changes from an arrow to a hand — that's how you can tell where the links are.

4. Select the Back button (or press Alt+left arrow) to return to the preceding page. This button (an arrow) is located in the upper-left corner of the screen (refer to **Figure 6-2**). Select the Back button to backtrack and revisit pages.

5. Select the Forward button (or press Alt+right arrow) to move forward to the page you visited in Step 3. The Forward button is next to the Back button (refer to **Figure 6-2**). Edge remembers the pages you visit to make it easy to go forward and back.

TIP

To zoom in and make a web page look bigger, press Ctrl+plus sign. To zoom out, press Ctrl+minus sign.

Back

Forward

Add This Page to Favorites

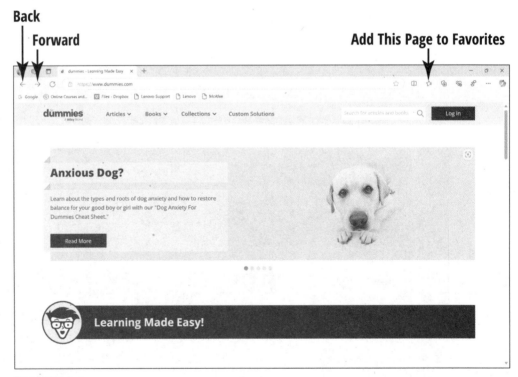

FIGURE 6-2

6. Select the Add This Page to Favorites button on the right side of the address bar (or press Ctrl+D). After you select this button, an Add to Favorites panel appears, as shown in **Figure 6-3**. Select the Add button to add Dummies.com to your Favorites list. Later in this chapter, "Bookmark and Revisit Your Favorite Websites" explains how to go to your favorite websites by selecting sites on the Favorites list.

TIP

You can change the text in the Add to Favorites panel before you select the Add button. However, there's usually no need to change the text unless it's overly long or unclear.

TIP

Browsing the web consists of entering addresses, following links, going forward and back, and revisiting your favorite websites. Relatively simple activities can absorb hours.

7. Keep Edge open if you want to go on to the next topic in this chapter.

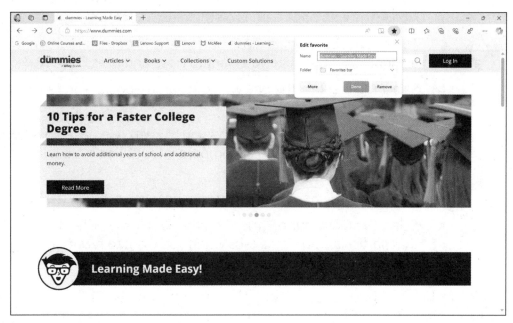

FIGURE 6-3

Open Multiple Pages in Separate Tabs

1. Open Edge if it isn't already open.

2. Go to the Google website at www.google.com. You can get there by typing www.google.com in the address bar and pressing Enter.

3. Select the New Tab button (or press Ctrl+T). This button is located to the right of the rightmost tab, as shown in **Figure 6-4**, **top**. A new web page appears, as shown in **Figure 6-4**, **middle**. What's more, a new tab (not coincidentally called New Tab) appears at the top of the screen.

4. On the new tab, enter **www.dummies.com** in the address bar and press Enter. You open the Dummies website on the second tab, as shown in **Figure 6-4**, **bottom**. Now, two websites are open in Edge. Google. com is open on the first tab; Dummies.com is open on the second. Notice the web page names on the tabs.

TIP To close a tab, select its Close button (the X) or make sure that you are looking at the page you want to close and press Ctrl+W.

5. Select the first tab, the one with the name Google. You return to the Google website.

Browsing in multiple tabs allows you to keep one page open while visiting another, perhaps to compare information or to follow a different thought.

TIP The keyboard shortcut for switching between tabs is Ctrl+Tab.

6. Select the Close button (the X) on the Dummies.com tab to close that particular tab. Close tabs when you want to reduce clutter and simplify switching among open tabs.

TIP The keyboard for closing the current tab is Ctrl+W. (*W?* Long story.)

Switch between tabs

New Tab | **New Tab button**

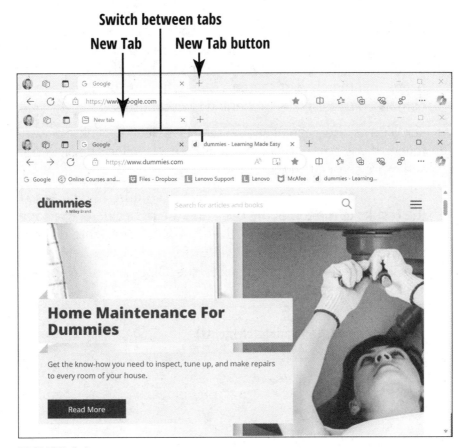

FIGURE 6-4

Search for Anything

1. With Edge open, go to the address bar and type **travel**. A drop-down list of search terms with the word *travel* appears as Edge attempts to guess what you're searching for. (Ignore this list for this exercise, but take advantage of it later.) Select Bing Search on the right side of the search term list to open the Bing website.

TIP

You can search the internet from the Search icon on the taskbar without opening Edge. Type a search term in the Search box. The Search panel lists items pertaining to the search term you entered, including ideas for web searches. Select a web-related item to search with Edge.

2. A search results page appears, as shown in **Figure 6-5**. The results come from www.bing.com, which is the default search engine for Edge. A *search engine* is simply a website that provides links to web pages that match your search. (That definition, however, ignores the complex process going on behind the scenes.)

3. Scroll down the page of search results. Select any link you want to follow. If you get to the bottom of the page, select the Next button to see more search results.

TIP

Some of the "search results" are advertisements. In Bing searches, the results at the top of the page and the right side of the page are paid for. Be careful of these advertisements, which are designed to sell you something, not to provide information. If you prefer not to see advertisements on web pages, see "Block Ads on Web Pages," later in this chapter.

Search results (and advertisements)

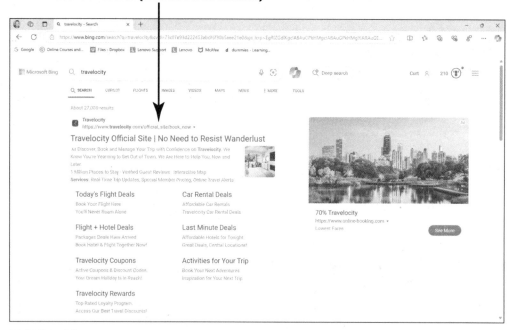

FIGURE 6-5

4. Return to the previous screen by selecting the Back button (or pressing Alt+left arrow).

5. Select the address bar and type **travel new mexico** (no capitals needed). As you type, potential matches for your terms appear in the drop-down list. If you see an item matching the search you want, select it in the list. Otherwise, press Enter.

TIP

Different search engines turn up different results. Other search engines include Google (www.google.com), Yahoo! (www.yahoo.com), and DuckDuckGo (www.duckduckgo.com). To use one of these search engines when exploring the web, enter its address in the address bar.

6. Note the tabs at the top of the Bing page, below the Search box. The first tab is All, which contains the results you see by default. Additional tabs vary with the search. Select each of the tabs, which may include any of the following:

   - **Images** displays pictures matching your terms.

   - **Videos** displays clips and snippets related to your search terms.

   - **Maps** will help you get there.

   - **News** displays search results from recent news, instead of all the results of the broader web.

   - **Shopping** directs you where to shop for items that match your search term.

7. Leave Edge open if you want to move on to the next topic.

Search Using Copilot AI

1. Copilot AI is built into Windows 11, and you can use it directly in Edge, as well. With Edge open, go to the address bar and type **most popular inexpensive travel destinations**. The search results appear (refer to **Figure 6-5**).

2. Instead of scrolling through the search results, you can switch to Copilot for a search response. Copilot will read search results for you and give you a concise answer. After searching for **most popular inexpensive travel destinations**, select the Copilot icon on the Copilot tab, shown in **Figure 6-6**.

3. Copilot will respond to your search and provide answers to your question. You can continue the Copilot conversation using the Ask Me Anything box at the bottom of the search results or switch to a different topic by clicking New Topic, shown in **Figure 6-7**.

TIP

You can find out more about using Copilot in Chapter 2.

Open Copilot

FIGURE 6-6

Copilot response

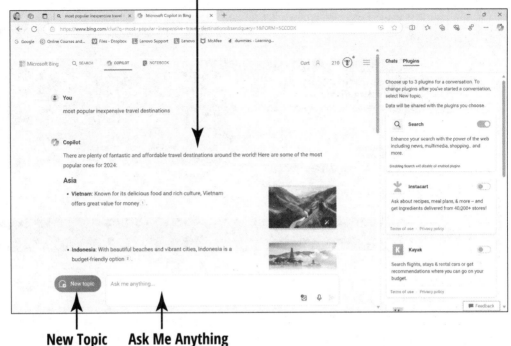

New Topic   **Ask Me Anything**

FIGURE 6-7

Bookmark and Revisit Your Favorite Websites

1. Open Edge, if it isn't already open, and go to your favorite website on the internet (or if you don't have a personal favorite, just go to www.dummies.com). If you've spent any time on the internet, you soon find websites that you want to visit again and again. Rather than memorize the addresses of these websites, you can add them to your Favorites list to make revisiting them quite easy.

2. Select the Add This Page to Favorites button (located on the right side of the address bar, it's shaped like a star). The Favorite Added dialog box appears. Accept the default website name or change it, then click Done, as shown in **Figure 6-8**. Use this panel to describe the websites you want to revisit and store their names in the Favorites panel (which you take a look at in Step 4).

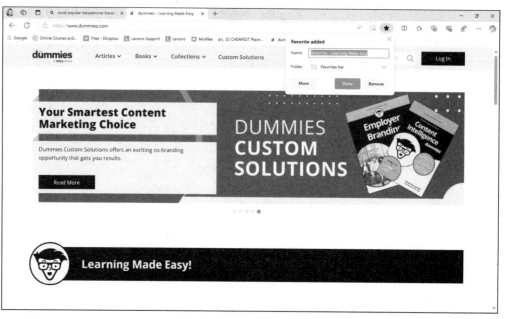

FIGURE 6-8

3. Before selecting the Add button to add your favorite website to the Favorites list, consider doing the following:

   - Enter a shorter, more concise, more descriptive name in the Name text box.

   - Open the Save In menu and select a folder name to store the website in a folder. (Step 8 explains how to create folders of your own.)

4. To verify that the website you are currently visiting has been added to the Favorites list, select the Favorites button (or press Ctrl+I). The Favorites panel opens, as shown in **Figure 6-9**. Look for your website in the Favorites panel.

5. Select the Back button to go to the website you visited previously. This button, a left-pointing arrow, is located in the upper-left corner of the screen. Next, select the Favorites button (or press Ctrl+I) and, in the list of bookmarked websites, select the website you bookmarked in Step 3 (refer to **Figure 6-8**). Your favorite website opens on the screen.

TIP

Don't hesitate to bookmark a website that you expect to revisit. Unless you bookmark it and add it to your Favorites list, you may not be able to find it again.

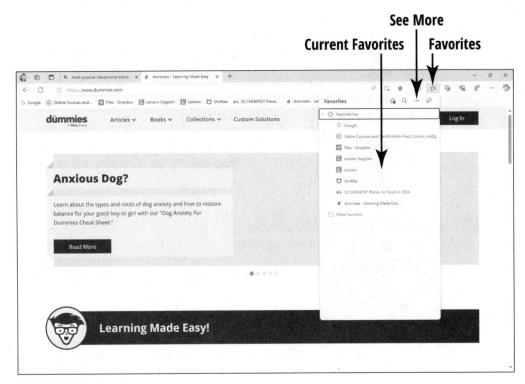

See More

Current Favorites **Favorites**

FIGURE 6-9

TIP

To remove a website from the Favorites list, display the Favorites list, right-click the website's name to display the context menu, and select Delete.

6. You can make the Favorites bar appear below the address bar, as shown in **Figure 6-10**. Merely by clicking or tapping a website name on the Favorites bar, you can go straight to a favorite website without having to open the Favorites panel. To display the Favorites bar, open the Favorites panel and select the See More button (refer to **Figure 6-9**). On the menu that appears, choose Show Favorites Bar. Any website you really, really like is a candidate for the Favorites bar.

7. Click anywhere onscreen except in the Favorites panel to close the Favorites panel. Then select the Favorites button to open the Favorites panel (refer to **Figure 6-9**). From here, you can manage websites that you have deemed your favorites:

   • **Reorder the websites and folders:** Drag a website or folder up or down in the Favorites panel until it lands in the right place.

- **Remove a website (or folder):** Display the folder or website's context menu (right-click or touch it with your finger). Then choose Delete.

- **Create a folder:** Choose Add Folder on the Favorites panel toolbar and type the new folder's name.

- **Rename a website (or folder):** Display the folder's context menu (right-click it or touch it with your finger), choose Rename, and enter a new name.

TIP

Folders can be a big help in organizing and finding bookmarks in the Favorites panel. If you're the type who likes to bookmark websites, give some thought to creating folders to store your bookmarks.

8. Leave Edge open if you want to move on to the next topic.

Favorites bar

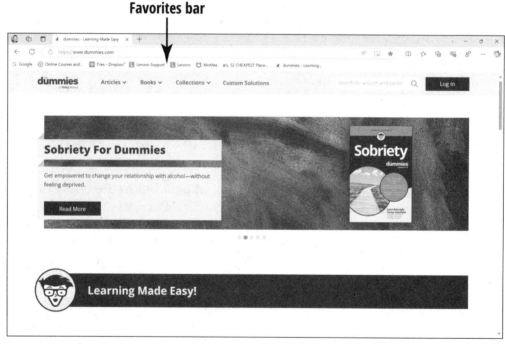

FIGURE 6-10

Explore Edge Features

1. You can decide what web pages you want to see on Edge's start screen. Go to your absolute favorite web page so that you can pin this web page to the Start screen. Select the Settings and More button (it's located in the upper-right corner of the screen and looks like three dots). Then, on the drop-down menu, choose More Tools and choose Pin to Start on the submenu. Select Pin in the confirmation dialog box that asks whether you really want to pin this web page to the Start menu or cancel. You get a second confirmation dialog box making sure, so click Yes to that box as well (yes, it's a bit redundant!).

2. Close Edge, then go to the Start screen, and select your favorite web page's tile. By selecting this tile, you do two things at one time — you start Edge and open it to your favorite website. Isn't that convenient?

3. Open Edge again. Select the Settings and More button, and then select History on the menu that appears. As shown in **Figure 6-11**, the History panel opens. This panel offers the means to back-track to websites you visited in the past hour, the past day, or the previous week.

4. Scroll to the bottom of the History panel to delve into ancient history and see websites you visited some time ago. Select a website to open it in Edge.

   To erase your browsing history and remove all web page names, select the Trash Can icon on the History panel.

TIP

5. Steps 3 and 4 demonstrate how Edge keeps track of web pages you visited, but what if you resent this kind of snooping? You can browse the web without letting Edge keep a historical record of the websites you visited. To browse in private, select the Settings and More button (it shows three dots and is located in the upper-right corner of the screen) and choose New InPrivate Window in the drop-down menu. Edge opens a second, "InPrivate" window, as shown in **Figure 6-12**. Websites you visit privately are not recorded in the History panel. Close the InPrivate window for now (or browse a while and then close it).

History button   Recent browsing history   Delete browsing data

FIGURE 6-11

FIGURE 6-12

TIP

You can tell when you're browsing privately because the word *InPrivate* appears in the upper-left corner of the Edge window (see **Figure 6-12**).

TIP

InPrivate browsing doesn't track your browsing history or associate searches with your profile; however, it does not hide your browsing from your school, employer, or internet service provider.

6. Have you ever found interesting things on the web, such as a photo, a recipe, or even a whole web page that you would like to save for later? You can do that with an Edge feature called Collections. Collections is a fun and easy to way to save anything you find on the web so that you can use it later. To get started, click the Collections button on the Edge toolbar and then click Next in the Collections panel, or, if you already have collections, select Create New Collection, as shown in **Figure 6-13**. You see a few screens with some basic info for you; just click Next through those screens.

Create New Collection   **Collections button**

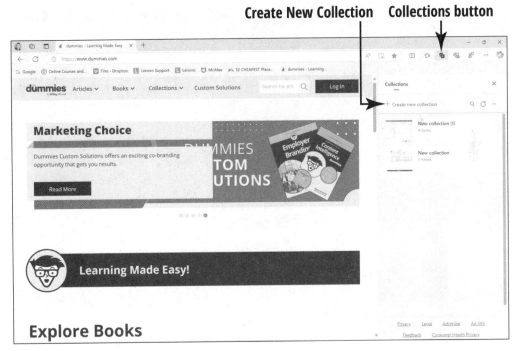

FIGURE 6-13

7. On the New Collection panel, you can add the current web page or even drag an image to the panel to begin a collection. In **Figure 6-14**, you can see some web pages and images in a collection.

Can't seem to drag an image to the Collections panel? Just right-click the image and select Add to Collections.

If you want to remove something from a Collection, point your mouse at the item, and a More Options menu appears in the right corner of the item. Select More Options and choose Remove

Items in the Collection

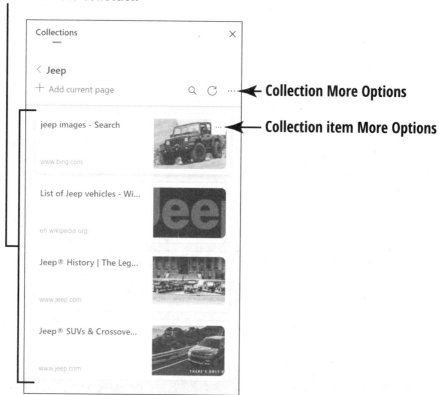

FIGURE 6-14

8. The Collection panel has an Add Note option, which is a handy feature. For example, if you're shopping for a new car and you save several websites and images, you can add your personal notes to the Collection so that you can review them later. Having a note can be a helpful way to remind you of specific details about images or websites that you don't want to forget. To add a note, select the More Options menu for the collection and choose Add Note.

9. You can create as many collections as you want. Select the Collections button and then select Create New Collection on the Collections panel. For example, you can create a collection of images and websites called Birthday Ideas, or maybe one called Recipes (if you like to cook), or Vacation Ideas. How you organize your Collections is completely up to you!

10. Close Edge or keep reading if you're inclined to find out how to turn off the ads on web pages.

Block Ads on Web Pages

1. As you soon find out, if you spend any time on the web, web pages are full of cumbersome advertisements. They often get in the way, and some even open pop-up windows that you have to close. How would you like to strip the ads from the web pages you visit? You can do that in two ways. First, you can turn on a pop-up blocking feature in Edge. Open Edge and select Settings and More. Then, choose Settings. In the Settings window in the left panel, select Cookies and Site permissions, shown in **Figure 6-15**. In the right panel, scroll down to All Permissions and select Pop-Ups and Redirects as well as Intrusive Ads to block them.

TIP

Depending on your computer's setup, these options may already be turned on, but be sure to check them!

Select Cookies and Site Permissions

Block Pop-Ups and Redirects and Intrusive Ads

Settings	Q Search settings
⊕ Profiles	
🔒 Privacy, search, and services	🎤 Microphone
◔ Appearance	Ask first
▭ Copilot and sidebar	((•)) Motion or light sensors
▤ Start, home, and new tab page	Allow sites to use motion and light sensors
⤺ Share, copy, and paste	🔔 Notifications
🍪 Cookies and site permissions	Ask first
🗔 Default browser	🗐 JavaScript
	Allowed
A⃗ Languages	
⤓ Downloads	🖼 Images
🕴 Accessibility	Show all
🖵 System and performance	
🎎 Family safety	◰ Pop-ups and redirects
🖶 Printers	Blocked
▯ Phone and other devices	🗐 Intrusive ads
↻ Reset settings	Blocked
	↻ Background sync
🜊 About Microsoft Edge	Allow recently closed sites to finish sending and receiving data
	⤓ Automatic downloads
	Ask when a site tries to download multiple files automatically

FIGURE 6-15

2. The second action you can take to stop ads is to install an Edge extension, which is a small piece of software. An ad-blocking extension can
help reduce the amount of ads you see as you search the web. You
can take a look at the ad blocking software that Microsoft recom-
mends at https://microsoftedge.microsoft.com/addons/search/
ad%20blocker. Check out the reviews of each and try installing one
for some additional ad blocking help.

TIP

Although ad blocking software and InPrivate browsing can help
you, know that some websites may not function properly or may
refuse to work altogether when you're using these tools. This
doesn't happen too often, but often enough to mention!

Chapter 7

Emailing Family and Friends

E very day, billions of email messages circle the globe, conveying greetings, news, jokes, even condolences.

Email also provides a way to send and receive *attachments*, such as documents or photos. Who needs faxes or postcards?

The Outlook app gives you access to email using your Microsoft account. Your Microsoft account can be associated with an email address from any email service provider, including Microsoft's own Outlook (www.outlook.com), Hotmail (www.hotmail.com), Live (www.live.com), or Xbox (www.xbox.com). You can also use email services such as Yahoo! (www.yahoo.com) and Gmail (www.gmail.com) without having a Microsoft account. You can easily set up these email services to work in the Windows 11 Outlook app, too, and this chapter shows you how.

In this chapter, you use the Outlook app for email. You compose, format, and send email, files, and pictures. You discover how to respond to incoming email. You also configure email accounts, and create and use email folders.

TIP

If you don't have a physical keyboard, see Chapter 1 for information on using the virtual keyboard.

Use the Outlook App

1. For email on Windows 11, select the Outlook icon on the taskbar. If you don't see the Outlook app on the taskbar, select the Search box on the taskbar and type **outlook** in the Search box. Select the Outlook app from the search results. Either way, the Outlook app opens. If you're currently signed in to your Microsoft account, the Outlook app knows your email address. (You gave it to Microsoft when you created the account.) This address is listed on the Outlook screen, and you're ready to go. If you're not currently signed in using a Microsoft account, enter your email address and password on the Sign In screen that appears and then select Sign In. (See Chapter 4 for information on creating a Microsoft account.)

TIP

The first time you use the Outlook app, you are invited to "add an account." In other words, Windows 11 offers its help linking an email account you have to the Outlook app. Select the Add Account button and follow the onscreen instructions for making an email account available to the Outlook app. See "Add an Email Account to Outlook," later in this chapter, for more information.

2. When you start the Outlook app, you land in the Inbox folder. If you haven't used your Microsoft account for email, you probably don't have any messages in your Inbox folder. Who would have written you already? You may, however, see a message or two from Microsoft.

3. On the Inbox screen, select the Expand/Collapse button next to your email address, as shown in **Figure 7-1**. The Folders panel expands, and you can see the names of all your folders in the Folders panel. In the Outlook app, email is kept in folders.

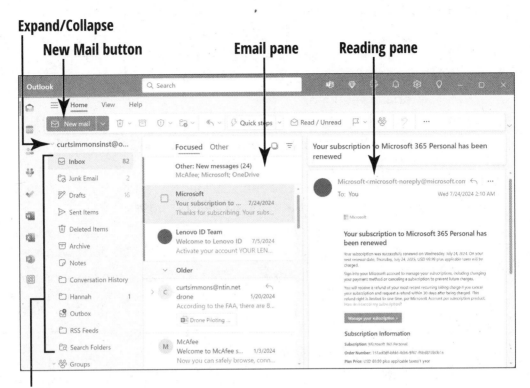

Expand/Collapse

New Mail button

Email pane

Reading pane

Folders

FIGURE 7-1

TIP

The number beside each folder name tells you how many unread email messages are in each folder.

4. Select any of the following folders in the Folders panel to see what email items are in each folder. The email in the selected folder appears in the Email pane, shown in **Figure 7-1**. You can select an email in the Email pane to read the email in the Reading pane, also shown in **Figure 7-1**.

- **Inbox:** Email you have received but not moved elsewhere appears here, including both read and unread email.

- **Junk Email:** Messages are moved to here — either automatically or by you — instead of to the Inbox, if they are suspected of being, well, *junk.* The more common term for unwanted email is *spam.* (It's a long story.) You may want to check this folder occasionally to see whether a message was misfiled here.

- **Drafts:** As you compose email (see the next section), you can save your message as a draft until you are ready to send it.

- **Sent items:** Copies of the email you send are stored here, appropriately enough.

- **Deleted items:** These are messages you have deleted from your Inbox. You can move messages out of the Deleted folder if you change your mind.

- **Archive:** The Outlook app provides this folder for email that you want to keep on hand for archival purposes.

- **Notes:** Notes in Outlook are like digital sticky notes: You can write down ideas, reminders, and anything else you don't want to forget.

- **Conversation History:** This folder contains conversations you have had with people through email. For example, if you and a friend email each other back and forth, the Conversation History folder keeps track of the entire conversation, which is much easier than keeping track of individual emails.

- **Outbox:** This consists of email you have sent or is in the process of being sent.

You may see other folders in the Folders panel besides the folders described here. For example, you can create additional folders to store specific groups of emails, and those folders will appear here as well.

5. Proceed to the next section, "Write an Email Message."

TIP

To search for stray email messages, go to the Search box on the Outlook toolbar and enter the content you're searching for. For example, enter a subject, sender, or something in the message.

Write an Email Message

1. To compose an email message in the Outlook app, select the New Mail button on the toolbar (refer to **Figure 7-1**). (It doesn't matter which folder you're in when you select this button.) The New Mail composition screen appears in the Reading pane, as shown in **Figure 7-2**.

2. In the To box, type an email address. If the Outlook app recognizes the address because you've sent email to or received email from the person to whom you're addressing your message, a pop-up box appears so that you can select the person's address without having to type it. Press the Tab key, touch the screen, or use the mouse to move to the next option.

TIP

To send email to more than one person at one time, select the Cc and Bcc button (located to the right of the address line). Then type a recipient's address in the Cc box (and the Bcc box as well, if you want to send a blind copy without revealing you've done so). (Once upon a time, *CC* stood for *carbon copy,* and then it became *courtesy copy.*) Technically, it makes no difference whether you use additional To addresses or the CC.

3. Enter a few words in the Subject box describing your message's content or purpose.

4. Select below the Subject line. Type your message. Avoid all caps; purists consider caps to be SHOUTING! No need to press Enter as you approach the end of the line — this isn't a typewriter.

TIP

Some people start a message with a salutation, such as *Hi Curt,* but many people do not. Some people sign email using their initials. Email can be as formal or casual as you choose to make it.

TIP

Words underlined with a red squiggle aren't recognized by Windows 11 and may be misspelled. Click the word to see a pop-up box with a correct spelling suggestion (there may be more than one). Choose the correct spelling if it is on the list. You can click Editor to see other suggestions as well.

5. When you're ready to send the message, select the Send button (you'll find it in the upper-left corner of the Compose window; refer to **Figure 7-2**). If you decide not to send the message, select the Discard button.

TIP

Email that you've composed but haven't sent yet is kept in the Drafts folder. You can postpone writing a message and finish it later by going to the Drafts folder and opening your message there. To go to the Drafts folder, select the Expand/Collapse button (if necessary) and then select Drafts in the Folders panel.

6. If you select the Send button, your message is sent and you return to the folder you were in at the beginning of Step 1.

7. Repeat from Step 1 as needed.

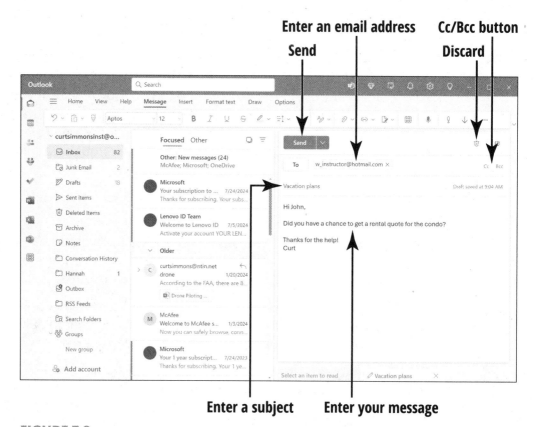

FIGURE 7-2

Format Email

1. If you want to add bold, italics, or other formats to email, select the text you want to fancy up in the Compose window, as shown in **Figure 7-3**. If no text is selected, your formatting will apply to the word in which the *cursor* (the blinking vertical line in the content) is located.

   - **Mouse:** Click and drag the mouse pointer over the text you want to select.

- **Touchscreen:** Tap and drag over the text you want to select.
- **Keyboard:** With the cursor at the beginning of the text you want to select, hold down the Shift key as you press the right or down arrow to select text. Release the Shift key only after you have completed your selection.

To apply formatting to one word, double-click or double-tap that word to select it and display the app bar in one step.

The keyboard shortcut to select all text is Ctrl+A. No mouse or touchscreen method is quite so complete.

2. Using the commands on the Format Text tab, you can choose several formatting options, such as the following:

- **Bold:** Bold is used for emphasis to make text stand out.
- **Italic:** Although italic can also be used for emphasis, it may be harder to read than normal or bold text.
- **Underline:** Because links are usually underlined automatically, you may want to avoid underlining text that isn't a link.
- **Bulleted list:** Select the Bullets button and enter items for the list. As you enter items, Outlook attaches a bullet point to the start of each line.
- **Numbered list:** Select the Numbering button and type the list. As you type, Outlook assigns a number to each line.
- **Styles:** Choose a style from the drop-down menu. A style applies many formats simultaneously. Heading 1, for example, enlarges the text and turns it blue.

See Chapter 1 for information on using the virtual keyboard's emoticons.

To create a hyperlink, go to the Insert tab and select the Link button. Then enter the address destination of the hyperlink in the address bar that appears. See Chapter 6 for more information about hyperlinks.

3. When you finish formatting the text, select the Send button.

Formatting toolbar   **Format Text tab**   **Select the text**

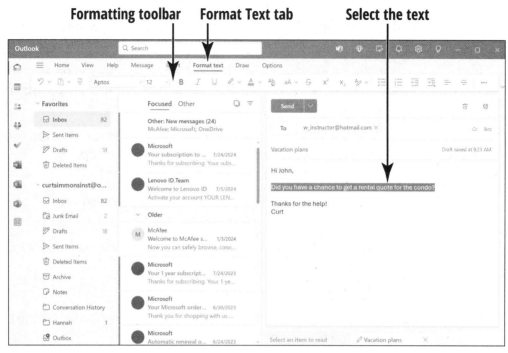

FIGURE 7-3

Send Files and Pictures

1. To send a file or picture with your email message, go to the Insert tab. As shown in **Figure 7-4**, the Insert tab offers tools for sending files and pictures.

2. Select the Attach File button to send a file. The Open dialog box appears. Locate and select the file you want to send and then select the Open button in the dialog box. You can send more than one file with an email message. In the Compose window, files you want to send appear as thumbnails the subject line (see **Figure 7-4**). Click the drop-down menu on a file and choose Remove Attachment if you change your mind about sending it.

3. To send a picture with an email message, place the cursor where you want the picture to be. Then select the Pictures button on the Insert tab. The Open dialog box appears. Select the picture and then click or tap the Insert button.

TIP

You can format pictures before sending them. Click or tap a picture to select it in the Compose window. The Picture Format tab appears. Using the tools on this tab, you can rotate, crop, and resize pictures.

4. When you have finished attaching your files and pictures, select the Send button to send them on their merry way.

FIGURE 7-4

TIP

Chapter 11 explains how you can use the Photos app to work with photos in Windows 11

Read and Respond to Incoming Email

1. Open the Outlook app using the taskbar icon or the Search box on the taskbar.

2. Select Inbox and then choose a message in the Inbox. The message appears in the Reading pane, as shown in **Figure 7-5**.

TIP

In email terminology, bouncing messages back and forth with some-one about the same subject is called a *conversation.* When you select an email message that is part of a conversation, the other messages in the conversation appear as well so that you can select and reread them. You can also find these conversations in the Conversation History folder.

3. After you read the message, you can respond to or forward it if you want. In the Reading pane, select the Reply or Reply All but-ton, which appears directly on the message (refer to **Figure 7-5**). You can also select the Reply button on the toolbar to see more options: Reply, Reply to All, or Forward. Selecting any of these options starts a new message (refer to **Figure 7-2**) that includes the text of the original message. The subject line is automatically *RE: [the original subject]* (in the case of replies) or *FW: [the original subject]* (in the case of forwarded messages). Complete your mes-sage and select the Send button.

TIP

Reply All sends your response to all the other recipients, if a mes-sage is addressed to more than one person. The Reply option sends your response only to the sender. Select Forward to send the selected message to someone else. You can add your own text or remove portions of the forwarded message in the process.

TIP

See the sections "Write an Email Message" and "Format Email," earlier in this chapter, for more information on composing an email message.

4. Note the following options for managing messages (to take advan-tage of additional options, select the More Options button at the end of the toolbar):

- **Delete:** Use this option to delete the message.

- **Set Flag:** Use this option to place a flag icon next to the message in the Inbox so that you remember to deal with the message later on. You can swipe right to flag a message.

- **Read/Unread:** Use this option if you want the message to appear unread (marked with a horizontal blue line in the Inbox).

Some people mark a message as unread when they want to deal with it later.

- **Move To:** Use this option to move the selected email from one folder to another. After you select Move To, select a folder in the drop-down menu that appears.

Manage a message using toolbar options   Selected message   Message content

Reply or Forward   More Options

Inbox   Reply, Reply to All

FIGURE 7-5

TIP

If you add email accounts from providers such as Gmail, you may see additional categories or options. See the section "Add an Email Account to Mail" at the end of the chapter.

Change Outlook Settings

1. In Outlook, display the Settings panel, shown in **Figure 7-6**. To display the Settings panel, select the Settings button (you find it on the top of the Outlook window with the other icons next to the Search box). The Settings window appears.

2. On the Accounts panel, select Accounts. You see any current email address that you have configured in Outlook. If you need to delete an old email address, select the Manage button for the email account. This action gives you two options (see **Figure 7-7**). You can remove the account here, or if you have several email addresses, you can set the email address as the primary account.

FIGURE 7-6

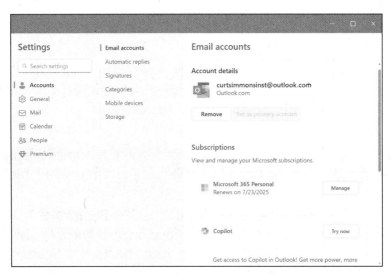

FIGURE 7-7

3. On the Settings window, you can also configure some additional items for your email (see **Figure 7-8**):

- **Automatic Replies:** If you'll be away from email for a period of time, you can turn on Automatic Replies. Outlook will reply to every message you receive with a message that you configure. You determine the start and end date and time and the message you want automatically sent (refer to **Figure 7-8**).

FIGURE 7-8

TIP

For your personal security, it's best to keep automatic reply messages short and vague. Say things like "I'm unavailable" and not "I'm out of the country on a wonderful vacation." You really don't want people knowing that your home is vacant for a period of time. Also, notice the check box option Send Replies Only to Contacts at the bottom of the window. This option is a good idea because it tells Outlook not to respond to emails from people you don't know.

- **Signatures:** Here, you can create a signature that includes any information you want, such as a business name, phone number, social media, and so on. You can choose to automatically apply the signature to new messages, replies, or both.

- **Categories:** You can create different color-coded categories for emails and calendar events so that they're easier to keep up with. For example, you can choose to always have your grandchild's email appear in blue, just to make sure you don't miss it! You can use categories to also apply to different work contacts or even calendar entries.

- **Mobile Devices:** You can download the Outlook app for your phone for free and then sync your Windows 11 Outlook app with your phone. This way, you get emails when you use Windows 11 and see them on the phone app as well. This capability is very convenient when you're on the go!

- **Storage:** Depending on the email you're using, you see some different options here, showing you how much email and data storage you have available. If you're using a Microsoft account, you can also add more storage here (for a fee, of course).

- **Download Email From:** You can limit how far back in time to go to download messages to your computer. This setting isn't relevant in a new email account.

- **Sync Options:** Turn the Email setting to Off only if you don't want the Outlook app to receive email from the account. Turn the other two settings, Calendar and Contacts, to Off if — for the purpose of privacy — you don't want the Outlook app to retrieve information from the Calendar app or People app.

Change Outlook's Layout and Appearance

1. Open Outlook's Settings window (select the Settings icon on the Outlook toolbar). Select General and then select Appearance (see Figure 7-9). Note that you choose light and dark modes and apply different images and themes to Outlook. These features give you a variety of appearances from which to choose. You can experiment with

any changes you want to make, and you can always return to this window and change settings back to the default if you're not happy.

2. In the General section, you can also make adjustments to the language and time, accessibility, how Outlook behaves when you're offline, and a few other options. These options are self-explanatory, so take a look.

3. Select Mail. Here you can make numerous adjustments to Outlook's settings, including Layout, Compose, Reply, Attachments, and many more. You don't have to do anything here, but if you'd like to change something about Outlook's interface, here's where you should look.

TIP

By default, Outlook sorts your Inbox messages using Focused and Other. This means that Outlook tries to guess which emails are the most important to you and put those in the Focused category. However, many people find this organizational method frustrating. So if you're thinking, "Outlook, just put my emails in my Inbox and leave them alone," you can turn off that feature by selecting Layout and then Focused Inbox. Select the Don't Sort My Messages radio button and, you'll be all set.

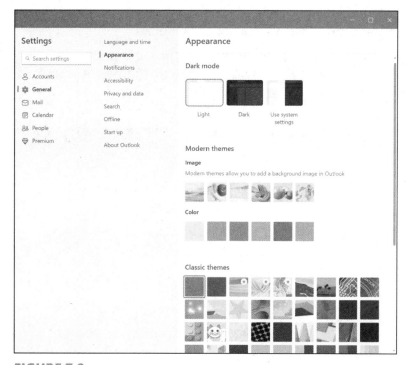

FIGURE 7-9

Add an Email Account to Outlook

1. If you have another email address, you can add it to Outlook. Adding an account has definite advantages. Instead of going hither and yon to collect your email from different accounts, you can collect all your mail in one place — the Outlook app. The following steps explain how to add an existing email account to Outlook. In Outlook, display the Settings panel (refer to **Figure 7-6**). Choose Accounts ⇨ Email Accounts and then select the Add account button.

TIP

Many people have more than one email address. Your internet service provider probably gave you an email account, and you may have another through work or school. However, if you use just one email address, you don't need to add another.

2. In the Add an Account dialog box, enter the email address you want to add and click Continue.

3. The system checks your email address and likely gives you another window. Click Continue.

4. The next screen informs you how your email account will connect with the Outlook app. You're asked to log in to the email account. Follow any additional instructions you see.

5. Return to the Email Accounts list in Settings. As shown in **Figure 7-10**, the Email Accounts window shows you the names of your accounts that are now configured in Outlook.

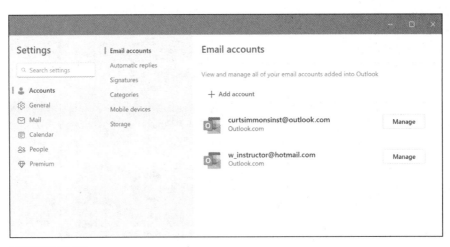

FIGURE 7-10

Create Email Folders

You may have a certain person with whom you exchange emails often, such as a friend, adult child, or even grandchild. If you want to keep these messages, you can create a custom folder just for that purpose. This way, you can easily access those emails any time you want.

1. In Outlook, right-click your email address in the left pane and choose Create New Folder.

2. A blank box appears in your folder list. Type a name for the folder Inbox and press Enter.

3. The new folder now appears in the folder list, as shown in **Figure 7-11**. If you change your mind, you can right-click a folder and choose Delete. However, any emails in the folder will also be deleted — just keep that fact in mind!

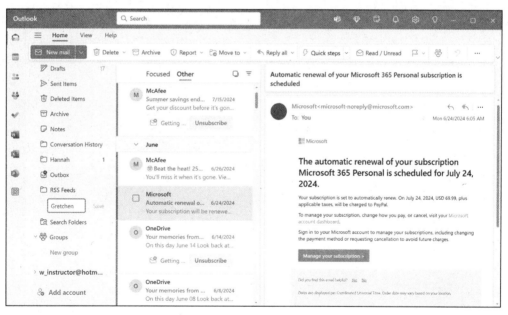

FIGURE 7-11

Organize Email in Folders

1. All email you receive initially appears in Outlook's Inbox. You can move email that you want to keep to an appropriate folder. (You can create as many folders as you like, as shown in the previous section.) To move an email, first select the email in the Inbox to open it.

2. On the toolbar, select Move to.

3. In the drop-down menu that appears, select the folder you want to move the email to.

TIP

If you move an email message to a folder but later want to move it to a different folder, you can easily do so. Just open the folder where the message is currently stored and repeat the previous steps to move it to a different folder.

IN THIS CHAPTER

» **Building a Community**

» **Chatting with People**

» **Connecting with family and friends**

» **Making video calls**

» **Setting up meetings**

Chapter **8**

Connecting with Microsoft Teams

K eeping in touch with family and friends is one of the most important things you can do. Windows 11 wants to make this easy for you with software called Microsoft Teams that is built into the operating system. Teams is, in a nutshell, communications software. Using Teams, you can easily chat with people you know, make video calls, and even schedule meetings.

Although the Teams software scales up to big, enterprise organizations where thousands of people in different locations can connect and work together, this chapter focuses on the Teams features that are most helpful to you.

TIP

When you first start Teams, the software may ask you questions about accessing your contacts and using your GPS or Wi-Fi location. It's best to allow these actions so that you don't have any limitations when you use Teams to connect with people. Also, you need to login with your Microsoft account when you first start Teams.

TIP

You can also download the Teams app and use the mobile app on your phone. That way, you can always stay in touch with people whether you're using your computer or your phone. The Teams app is free — just search for it on your phone's app store.

Build a Community

1. On the taskbar, enter **Teams** in the Search box and click the result that appears to open the Teams app. The Teams app consists of a simple interface with four button options on the left toolbar: Activity, Community, Chat, and Calendar. Select the Community option, as shown in **Figure 8-1**.

2. A community is a group of people you connect with for a specific purpose. For example, you can create a community that includes all your family members, or a community for a neighborhood organization, a school group, a volunteering group, and so forth. Note that you don't have to create a community to use Teams, but a community helps group different people together. Choose the Create My Own option, shown in **Figure 8-1**.

3. In the Create Your Community window, enter a name and description of the community you're creating. Notice the option for requiring approval before someone can join the community. As a security step, it's a good idea to turn this feature on, shown in **Figure 8-2**. When you're done entering information, click the Create button.

4. Your community now appears in the Community section of Teams. From here, you can create a new message, post files, and photos, create events, and most importantly, invite people to your community. Click the Invite Members button, shown in **Figure 8-3**, and add email addresses and phone numbers of the people you want to invite. Teams will send those people emails or text messages so that they can join the community. After people join your community, you can interact with them through chatting and video calls.

Community

FIGURE 8-1

FIGURE 8-2

Invite Members

FIGURE 8-3

TIP

Your community page displays a banner graphic at the top. You can change this graphic to any image you like. Click the Edit icon, shown in **Figure 8-4**, on the image to select a new image or upload your own.

Edit banner image

FIGURE 8-4

Chat in Teams

1. On the taskbar, enter **Teams** in the Search box and click the result that appears to open the Teams app. If you have community, select the Community button on the left toolbar, or select the Chat.

2. After you select Chat, shown in **Figure 8-5**, you can select an existing contact, or you can invite new contacts directly on this window. You can respond to any previous chats or start a new chat by selecting the contact and typing the chat.

3. New chats appear in the contents pane (see Figure 8-5). As you chat, notice you can add images, emojis, and files to your chat, just as you would an email or text message. When you complete a message, click the Send button.

FIGURE 8-5

TIP

If you're chatting with someone, you can easily jump to a video call by clicking the Meet Now button (see **Figure 8-6**). See the "Start a Meeting" section, later in this chapter.

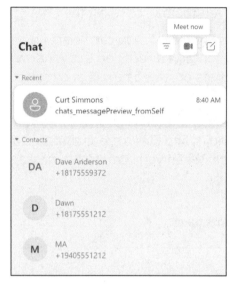

FIGURE 8-6

Respond to Activity

1. In Teams, select Activity on the left toolbar. The Activity section shows you specific mentions (Teams calls them @mentions) of you. For example, you may be chatting with five people in a group. When someone specifically mentions you, that mention appears in Activity, as shown in **Figure 8-7**. This feature helps make sure you don't miss anything specific to you.

TIP

When someone mentions you, or you mention someone, you type *@username*. For example, if you have a contact named Sue Williams and you want to mention Sue, you type **@Sue Williams**. Your mention then shows up in Sue's Activity in Teams. Note that a mention has an @ symbol with it and is pronounced "at mention."

2. With Activity selected on the toolbar, click the @mention that you want to see in the Feed (navigation pane). Then you can respond to the @mention in the content pane (see **Figure 8-7**).

3. @mentions appear in the Feed in bold type, meaning that you haven't read them yet. You can mark an @mention as read after you read it, or if you don't want to read it, just point to the @mention and select More Options to the right. You see the option to mark the @mention as read (see **Figure 8-8**).

FIGURE 8-7

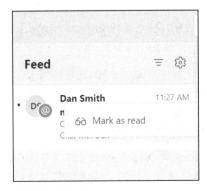

FIGURE 8-8

Manage Chats

1. In Teams, select Chat on the toolbar.

2. Choose a chat conversation in the navigation pane and select More Options (point your mouse to the chat to see the More Options button appear; it's the three dots).

3. The More Options menu gives you a few different ways to manage chat conversations, as shown in **Figure 8-9**:

   - **Open Chat in New Window:** This option opens the chat in a new, pop-out window.

   - **Mark as Read/Unread:** You can mark a chat as either read or unread. If you've read the chat, it will default to "read," but you can change it back to unread if you want (which is a good way to remind yourself to respond to chat later).

   - **Pin:** This option pins the chat conversation to the top of your Chat list in the navigation pane. Doing so makes it easy to return to conversations you're actively engaged in.

   - **Mute:** Say you're chatting with a group of friends, but the conversation spirals into details that don't pertain to you. You can mute the conversation so that you don't get updates as people continue to chat.

   - **Hide:** This option hides the chat from the navigation pane so that you won't see it any longer.

   - **Delete:** Finished with a chat? You can choose to delete it from the navigation pane. Be careful: After you delete a chat conversation, it's gone forever!

4. You can also filter your chat conversations. For example, if you have a lot of conversations in the chat navigation pane, it can be difficult to find the one you want. You can select the Filter option on the navigation pane and see only the chats from a specific person, as shown in **Figure 8-9**. The Filter option will make finding specific chat conversations easier.

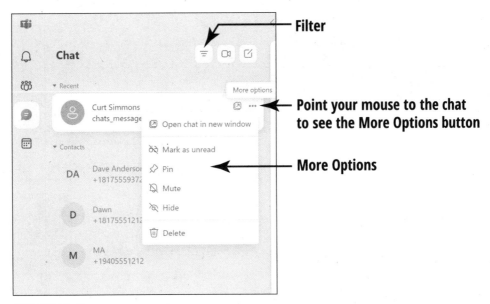

Filter

Point your mouse to the chat to see the More Options button

More Options

FIGURE 8-9

Start a Meeting

1. In Teams, a *meeting* is a live video call that you make over the internet. To start a meeting, select Chat on the toolbar and select the Meet Now button, shown in **Figure 8-10**.

2. In the dialog box that appears, give the meeting a name (you can accept the default name). You can then get a link for the meeting, which you can send to others whom you want to attend, or you can start the meeting. Click Start Meeting.

3. The Teams interface changes to a video meeting window, shown in **Figure 8-11**. Before you join the meeting, you can set a few important settings here:

   - **Mic:** This setting is on by default; otherwise, your microphone will not work during the meeting.

   - **Camera:** This setting is on by default; otherwise, your webcam will not work during the meeting.

Meeting Name and Start Meeting

Meet Now

FIGURE 8-10

Camera

More **Mic**

FIGURE 8-11

- **More:** This option, shown in **Figure 8-12**, gives you some different video effects so that you can blur or change the background of your video. Select More and choose Video Effects and Settings. This option is helpful to reduce clutter and increase visibility in your video. It also helps provide some level of privacy (unless you want everyone to see the unfolded laundry behind you!). Select a background option and select Apply.

- **Device Settings:** To make adjustments to the camera or mic settings, click the down arrow next to the camera or mic icon on the toolbar. A drop-down menu appears where you can make selections. For example, under Camera, you can adjust the brightness and focus, as shown in **Figure 8-13**. You may not need to make any adjustments, but if you do, it's good to have a few options here.

4. As other participants join the meeting, you see them on your screen. Now you can visit virtually with your friends, family, and any other person or group you want to meet with.

Select More and choose Video Effects and Settings

Choose a background option and select Apply

FIGURE 8-12

Choose the drop-down menu next to Camera or Mic

FIGURE 8-13

When you're finished meeting, just select the red Leave button in the upper-right corner of the screen.

TIP

Schedule a Meeting

1. In Teams, select Calendar on the left toolbar and choose the New Meeting button, shown in **Figure 8-14**. The odds are good that you'll want to schedule meetings with other people. When you schedule a meeting, you create a date and time and then send a meeting link to the people you want to invite so that you can all meet at the same time. This is a great way to schedule time with others.

Select calendar

Select New Meeting

FIGURE 8-14

2. In the New Meeting window, make sure that your time zone is correct, and then enter the details of the meeting, as shown in **Figure 8-15**. When you're done, select Save.

3. Teams creates the meeting and gives you a dialog box from which you can copy the meeting link and even add it to Google Calendar. Either way, you want to share the meeting with the link or calendar with the people you want to attend.

TIP

When you send a meeting link, all the participant has to do is click the link to open the meeting in Microsoft Teams.

TIP

Need to cancel a meeting? No problem — select Calendar on the toolbar and locate your meeting on the calendar. Right-click the meeting and select Cancel. You can also right-click the meeting and choose Edit to change the date, time, and other details.

Enter meeting details   **Select Save when you're done**

FIGURE 8-15

Manage Teams Settings

1. In Teams, select Settings and More and choose Settings from the menu, as shown in **Figure 8-16**.

2. In the Settings pane, choose Notifications and Activity. Teams will notify you if someone is trying to connect with you through notifications and sounds. Here, you can determine what notifications you receive. For more information about Windows 11 notifications, see Chapter 3.

3. Select Appearance and accessibility in the Settings panel. Here, you can choose a theme for Teams. By default, the theme follows the current Windows operating system theme, but you can use the drop-down menu to change it to other options such as Light, Dark, and High Contrast, as shown in **Figure 8-17**.

4. Select Privacy in the Settings panel. The default settings here are all you need, but you should note one setting. By default, when you read a chat or anything else in Teams, the sender can see that you've read it (called a read receipt). You can turn this feature off with the toggle button if you don't want others knowing whether you've read their messages.

FIGURE 8-16

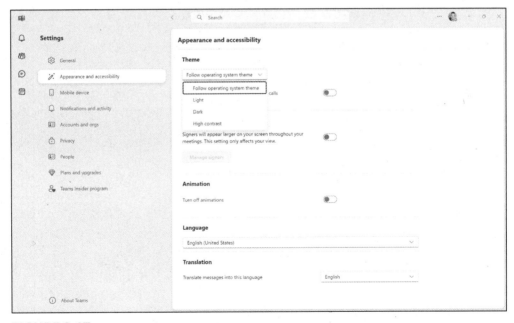

FIGURE 8-17

Chapter **9**

Exploring Apps for Your Daily Life

T his chapter describes a handful of apps that the average Joe or Jane might use every day. It shows how to manage tasks and lists to keep track of your life with the To Do app. You also use the Calendar feature in Outlook to keep track of birthdays, anniversaries, appointments, and other events.

This chapter delves into the Maps app, showing you how to use it to get directions and to look up hotels and restaurants when you're on the go. You see how two Windows 11 apps, Sticky Notes and Alarms & Clock, can help you complete tasks on time.

Finally, this chapter demonstrates how to make the Lock screen indicate whether you've received email, how to chat face-to-face with family and friends over the internet with Skype, and how to use the Journal app.

Add a Task with Microsoft To Do

1. Select the Search box on the taskbar and search for *To Do.* Select the To Do app that appears in the search results. The To Do app opens, probably with the Getting Started option selected in the left pane. If not, select Getting Started, shown in **Figure 9-1**.

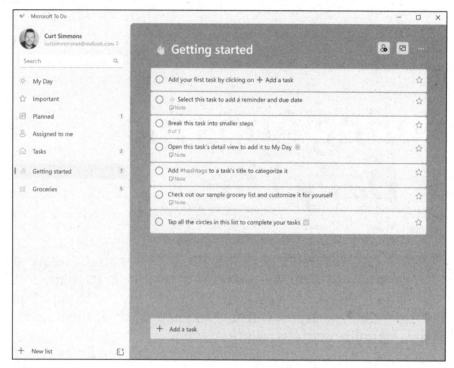

FIGURE 9-1

2. Select Add a Task in the right pane. Type the name of the task. For example, you could type **Pay phone bill**, as shown in **Figure 9-2**.

3. After you type a name, three options appear in the name field: Add a Due Date, Remind Me, and Repeat (refer to **Figure 9-2**). Select Add a Due Date, shown in **Figure 9-3**, and select one of the options, or choose pick a date to choose a date from a calendar.

4. To set a reminder, select the Remind Me option and choose a default reminder time to appear, or you can pick a date and time. When you select a reminder, Windows 11 displays a reminder on your computer on the designated date and time.

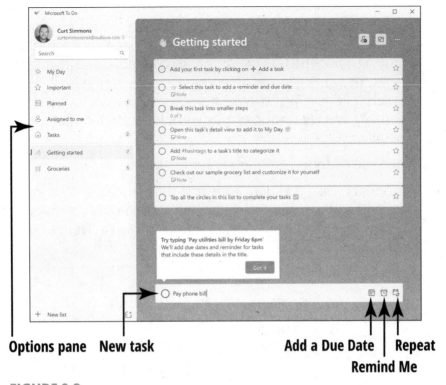

Options pane   New task

Add a Due Date | Repeat

Remind Me

FIGURE 9-2

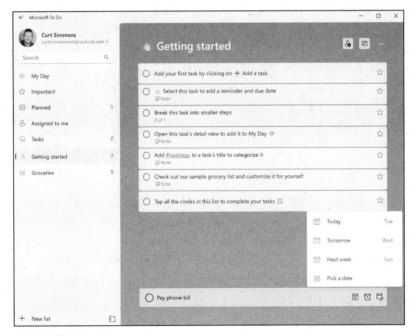

FIGURE 9-3

5. If you want to make the task recurring, select the Repeat option. This feature is handy for tasks you do every week or month, such as paying a bill. The task will automatically recur, and if you set up a reminder, you'll also get an automatic reminder as well. When you select Repeat, just choose how often you want to repeat the task (daily, weekly, and so on), or you can create a custom repeat schedule.

6. When you're done, just press Enter to save it

7. Tasks that have a due date appear in the Planned section in the left pane of the app. If you select Planned, you see a list of tasks that you've created and when they're due, as shown in **Figure 9-4**.

FIGURE 9-4

When you finish a task (or decide you don't want it any longer), just select the circle next to the task's name. This will make the task show as completed.

TIP

Edit a Task

1. Sometimes things change and you need to edit a task as well. For example, say you have an appointment that gets moved to a different day or time. You don't need to create a new task — you can just edit the existing one quickly and easily. Open the To Do app and locate the task you want to edit (you may find it by selecting Planned or Tasks in the left pane).

2. Select the task you want to edit. A pop-up panel appears with options to edit the task. For example, in **Figure 9-5**, Curt has an appointment to take the cat to the vet. He can simply select the date to change it and save the new date.

3. You can also change the Remind Me schedule or the Repeat schedule on this pane. Just select those options to edit them.

4. Change your mind and want to delete a task completely? No problem — just right-click the task and select Delete Task.

FIGURE 9-5

Create a List

Individual tasks are helpful, but sometimes you need a group of tasks that revolve around the same thing. In this case, you want to create a To Do List. For example, say you're planning a birthday party for a family member and have several ideas you don't want to forget. A list can help you remember them!

1. Open the To Do app and in the left pane, select New List. Type a name for the list and press Enter. The new list appears. **Figure 9-6** shows a list created to plan a birthday party.

2. Begin adding tasks to the list by adding an item to the response box at the bottom of the new task's pane (shown in **Figure 9-6**). After you create one task, this box changes to say Add a Task. Click in the box again and type an additional task. You can create as many tasks as you need for your list. The tasks appear under the list name, as shown in **Figure 9-7**.

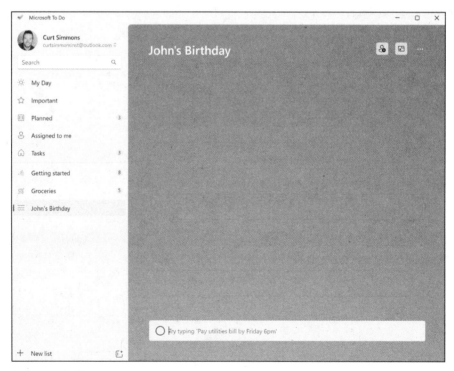

FIGURE 9-6

3. You can make changes to any task in a list as needed. You can complete a task, edit it, or even delete it if you want. Refer to the previous "Edit a Task" section.

FIGURE 9-7

TIP

You can do other things with the To Do app, such as plan your day, flag important tasks, and manage groceries, but everything in the app revolves around Tasks and Lists, so feel free to explore the app a bit more. Also, you can download the Microsoft To Do app on your phone, and it will sync with your computer's To Do List automatically (if you're signed in with your Microsoft account). Just search for Microsoft To Do at your app store to find and download it. The mobile app is a great tool when you need a list of to-do items at your fingertips or reminders about groceries you need — after all, you don't want to forget the ice cream!

Add an Event to the Outlook Calendar

1. To see the calendar and add events, open the Outlook app by selecting the Search box on the taskbar, typing **outlook** in the Search box, and selecting Outlook in the search results. You may also see the Outlook app icon on your taskbar.

TIP   Windows 11 also uses Outlook for email. Find out more about using Outlook for email in Chapter 7.

2. In Outlook, select Calendar on the left vertical toolbar (refer to **Figure 9-8**). You can choose which month you would like to view, but you can also use the toolbar to specifically choose the following:

   - **Day:** This format displays a single day with a box for each hour. Select arrows near the top of the screen to scroll back or forward one day at a time. Scroll up and down to see more hours in the day.

   - **Work Week:** The current work week appears (Monday – Friday). Scroll or use the arrows to go from hour to hour or week to week.

   - **Week:** The current week appears (Sunday through Saturday). Scroll or use the arrows to go from hour to hour or week to week.

   - **Month:** The current month appears in the classic month layout. (Depending on the size of your screen, you may have to scroll to see this format.) Today is highlighted with a different color. Use arrows near the top to move forward and back a month at a time.

3. The Calendar offers two ways to add an event: the short-but-cursory way and the slow-but-thorough way:

   - **Short but cursory:** Click or tap the day on which the event is to occur (in the Month format) or the hour and date on which it is to occur (in the Day or Week formats). You see the pop-up window shown in **Figure 9-9**. With luck, this little window is all you need to describe the event. Type the event's name, and if it isn't an all-day event, deselect the All Day check box (if necessary) and use the start time and end time menus to describe when the event starts and ends. You can also type the event's location. Select the Save button when you finish describing the event (or select the More Details link to open the Details screen and go to Step 4).

Calendar **Toolbar options**

FIGURE 9-8

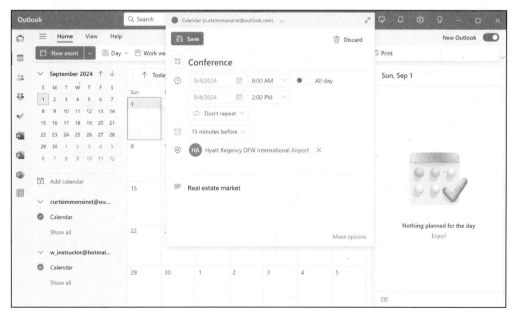

FIGURE 9-9

- **Slow but thorough:** Select the New Event button (refer to **Figure 9-8**). The Details window appears, as shown in **Figure 9-10**. Move on to Step 4.

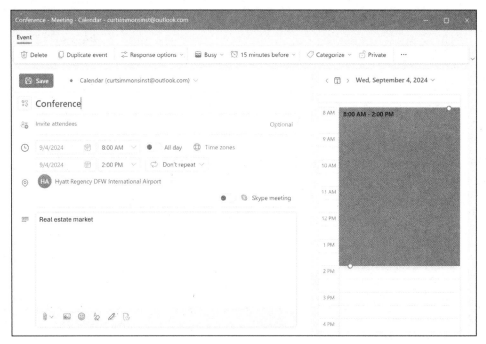

FIGURE 9-10

4. Enter (or change) any of the following data for the event:

- **Event Name:** Describe the event in one to three words. The description you enter will appear on your calendar.

- **Location:** If listing the location will help you get to the event on time, by all means list it. The location, like the event name, appears on the calendar.

- **Start and End:** Select the calendar icon, and on the pop-up menu that appears, choose the day on which the event begins and then the day on which it ends.

- **Hours/All Day:** If this isn't an all-day event, deselect the All Day check box, if necessary. Then use the drop-down menus to describe when the event will occur.

TIP

If the event is one that recurs, you can schedule it on a weekly, monthly, or yearly basis on the calendar. Weekly staff meetings, birthdays, and anniversaries are examples of recurring events. Select the Repeat button on the app bar along the top of the screen to schedule a recurring event. Then, using the Repeat options that appear in the Details screen, describe how often the event occurs, when it occurs, and when it will cease occurring.

- **Event Description:** Describe the event in detail if you think it's necessary. Should you wear the tux or the zoot suit? The ball gown or the formal dress? This is the place to record your thoughts on the matter.

5. Optionally, use the commands on the app bar at the top of the screen to further describe the event:

- **Delete/Duplicate event:** You can quickly delete an event or you can duplicate it, which is a helpful feature if the event is basically the same event but on another day.

- **Reminder:** How far in advance of the event do you want Calendar to display a notification? Choose options on the drop-down menu such as Don't Remind Me, 5 Minutes, 15 Minutes, 30 Minutes, 1 Hour, 12 Hours, 1 Day, or 1 Week. You can even have Outlook send you an email reminder.

- **Private:** Select this option (look for the lock symbol) to prevent this event from appearing on a shared or public calendar. The event remains visible on your own screen.

6. When you're done, select the Save button.

7. On the calendar, your event appears on the specified date and time.

8. To edit an event, select it on the calendar. A pop-up screen appears with details about the event. Select the event's name in the pop-up screen to open the Details screen, where you can add or change any detail.

TIP

You can quickly delete an event by clicking it on the calendar and choosing the Delete option on the pop-up screen.

TIP

If your Microsoft account is connected to a third-party service such as Gmail, events from that service appear on your calendar. Outlook is good about picking up any events connected to your email address, such as deliveries, airline reservations, and such. This feature is helpful because you don't have to manually add these items — they automatically appear on your calendar.

Search and Explore with the Maps App

1. Use the Search box on the taskbar and search for Maps; then select the Maps app in the search results. Use this app to locate places and to get driving or walking directions.

TIP

If you can't find the Maps app on your computer, download Windows Maps from the Microsoft Store (it's free). See Chapter 10 for more information about the Microsoft Store.

2. Click or tap in the Search box. A drop-down list appears. It lists items you already searched for, if you searched already. You can select an item on the list to revisit it.

3. Type **victory park, dallas** (you don't need to enter capital letters) in the Search box. As you type, options appear in the Search panel. Select the address you entered, not the names of businesses located at the address. As shown in **Figure 9-11**, the Maps app shows you where the address is located; it also provides a photo. In addition to typing addresses in the Search box, you can enter the names of places and landmarks.

4. Select the Zoom Out button (or press Ctrl+minus sign) on the app bar in the map. Then select the Zoom In button (or press Ctrl+plus sign). The tools on the app bar can help you read the map better (refer to **Figure 9-11**).

5. Select the Directions button (refer to **Figure 9-11**), which is the button in the upper-right corner near the Search box. (Or you can press Ctrl+D.) Tools appear to help you get from place to place. Click or tap in the Starting Point box (Box A), and when the drop-down menu appears, choose **Victory Park**, the address you already entered. In the Destination box (Box B), enter **n lamar st**.

Find restaurants, hotels, and more   Zoom in or out

FIGURE 9-11

6. Select the **Get Directions** link. As shown in **Figure 9-12**, the Maps app gives you several sets of driving directions between the two addresses and tells you how long each drive will take. Select a drive in the list to get specific instructions for driving between the two addresses. After you select a drive, you can click or tap the Print icon to print the instructions.

7. Are you walking, not driving? In that case, select the Walking icon at the top of the Search panel to get directions for walking between the two locations. You can also select the Transit icon to get directions for getting there by public transportation.

8. The Maps app keeps tabs on your travels. Select a tab along the top of the screen to retrace your steps and revisit a map you saw earlier.

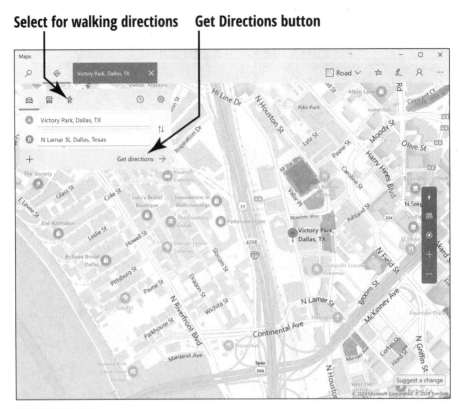

Select for walking directions **Get Directions button**

FIGURE 9-12

Stay on Time with the Clock App

1. For the most part, the Clock app is a simple tool that gives you a few different options to set timers. Open the Clock app by searching for Clock, using the Search icon on the taskbar. You see a navigation pane on the left side of the app where you can toggle between different options (see **Figure 9-13**). They are

    • **Focus Sessions:** You can choose Start Focus Session to create a timer for something specific. For example, if you're exercising on a treadmill and you want to walk for a specific time, you can create daily focus sessions and track your progress over time (refer to **Figure 9-13**).

- **Timer:** You can activate some present timers (1 minute, 3 minutes, 5 minutes, and 10 minutes). You can also click the + icon to create a new timer. When you start a timer, a chime will sound when the timer is complete.

- **Alarm:** You can set a daily alarm (or choose which days you want the alarm to sound). For example, you could set a daily wake-up alarm, a daily exercise alarm, and so forth.

Alarm

Timer

Focus Sessions

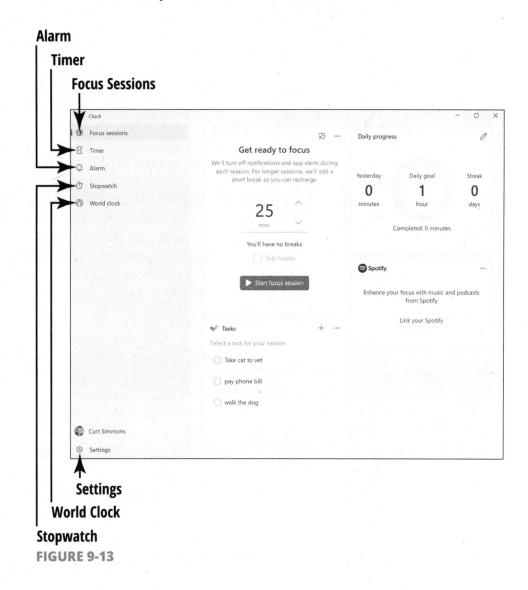

Settings

World Clock

Stopwatch

FIGURE 9-13

- **Timer:** Here you find a simple timer you can use. You can also select the Lap/Split button while you're using the timer to mark laps and such. This feature is helpful if you're exercising and want to flag the time a lap took to complete.

- **World Clock:** This lets you view the local time, but you can also select the + button to see the time and date in any city in the world.

2. You can select the Settings option (refer to **Figure 9-13**) to make some adjustments to the Clock app. For example you can turn on or off end-of-session or break sounds (and adjust the sounds as well). You can also adjust the app theme if you like.

Write with Notepad

1. Windows 11 comes with a text editor, which is a simple word pro-cessing app, called Notepad. Word processors are applications that you can use to write letters, reports, and other documents. Notepad lets you write text, but it doesn't do much of anything else compared to Microsoft Word, the world's most famous word processor. But Notepad doesn't cost anything. To start Notepad, enter **notepad** in the Search box on the taskbar and then select Notepad in the search results. Notepad opens, as shown in **Figure 9-14**.

2. Type a sentence or two in Notepad. You'll notice there is no toolbar for formatting any text, such as choosing fonts, font sizes, or com-mands such as bold, italic, and so forth. Remember, Notepad is just a basic text editor. The good news is that the spell checker is automati-cally turned on, so if you misspell a word, that word will be under-lined in red. For example, in **Figure 9-14**, "beautiful" is misspelled, so Notepad has underlined the word in red.

3. Select the Edit menu. Here, you can perform basic text-management tasks, such as copying and pasting. You can also search for words or phrases in your text and automatically insert the time and date on which the text was written.

4. Select the View menu, which enables you to zoom in or out. By default, the Status bar and Word wrap (which sends words down to the next line instead of hyphenating them) are turned on. You can select those options to turn them off if you like.

5. Press Ctrl+S or choose File ⇨ Save (located in the upper-left corner of the screen) to save your document. You see the Save As dialog box. Notepad documents are saved as basic text files. Any computer can open and read basic text files, so you can easily share them with someone else if you like.

FIGURE 9-14

Chapter 15 explains how to open, save, and otherwise manage files.

TIP

Write a Sticky Note to Yourself

1. In the Search box, enter **Sticky Notes**. Select the Sticky Notes app in the search results to open it. A sticky note — like the ones in **Figure 9-15** — appears on the screen. Sticky notes are the digital equivalents of the yellow stick-'em tabs that people attach to their

computers and desks. Use sticky notes to remind yourself to do something or be somewhere.

2. Type the note. Then move the pointer over the stripe at the top of the note and drag the note to a corner of the screen.

TIP

You can change the size of a sticky note. Move the pointer over the lower-right corner of the note. When the pointer changes to double arrows, start dragging.

3. Click or tap the New Note button (refer to **Figure 9-15**). Another sticky note appears. Write a second note and drag it to a corner of the screen.

4. Click or tap the Delete Note button on one of your notes when you no longer need it. You can also format the note text or even add an image (refer to **Figure 9-15**).

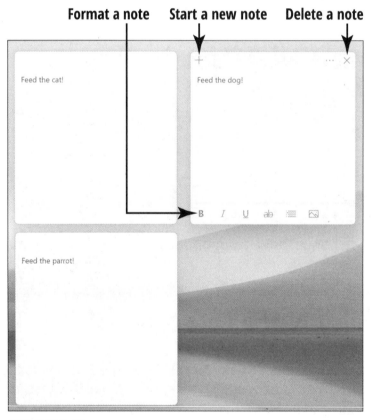

FIGURE 9-15

Chat Face-to-Face with Skype

1. Select the Search box on the taskbar and type **skype** in the Search box; then select the Skype app in the search results. You can use this app to video chat with others. (You can also use the Microsoft Teams app to video chat; see Chapter 8 for more information.) You may need to download Skype from the Microsoft Store. See Chapter 10 to find out more about using the Microsoft Store. (Don't worry; the Skype app is free.) To use Skype, your computer must have audio and video capability. You can also use Skype if a webcam is connected to your computer.

TIP

You need to sign in to your Microsoft account before you use Skype. See Chapter 4 for information about creating a Microsoft account.

2. The first time you use the Skype app, the screen asks you to sign in with your Microsoft account as well as add a photo (if you like), and then it asks you to test your microphone and webcam. Just follow the instructions to check everything.

3. The Skype screen lists the names of people on your Contacts list and people you have called before using Skype. You can select one of these people to call them now. If the person you want to call isn't listed, enter their name in the Search Skype box and select the Search button (which looks like a magnifying glass). The Skype directory opens, as shown in **Figure 9-16**. Scroll to find the person you want to call, using the person's photo ID and geographical information as your guide. You may also see Copilot in your recent chats. If you've used Copilot before, it shows up here, and you can interact with Copilot directly in Skype.

4. When you see the name of the person you want to call, select the name. Then, on the call screen, select the Video Call button. You hear a ring tone as the call is made, and you see the person's face if they answer. Your face appears in the lower-right corner of the screen so that you can see what your face looks like to the caller. (You can drag this screen from place to place.) Start talking. Smile. Trade the latest news. Have a ball.

Search   **Create a new contact**

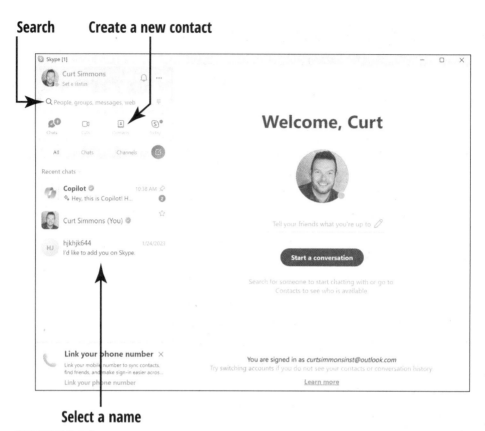

Select a name

FIGURE 9-16

TIP

Select the Video and Microphone buttons when you need a little privacy. Select the Video button to turn off your video (the other caller can't see you); select the Microphone button to turn off your audio (the other caller can't hear you).

TIP

Select the Open Conversation button (in the upper-right corner of the screen) to send an instant message to the other caller. The message panel appears. In the bottom of the message panel, type your message and press Enter. Sending text messages is a useful way to communicate when you have technical difficulties or the other caller isn't answering. Select the Close Conversation button (at the top of the Chat window) to close the message panel.

5. Select the red End Call button to complete your call.

6. When someone calls you, the Incoming Call panel appears. Select Turn Video On (at the bottom of the panel) to initiate the call.

Create with the Journal App

1. Select the Search box on the taskbar and type **journal**; then select the Journal app in the search results. The Journal app is a great place to manually write any kind of content that you want. You can even include photos in your journal entries. Note that the Journal works only with a stylus (a pen-like input device). You can't use a keyboard or your finger with the app.

2. In the Journal app window, select New Journal. Give the journal a name; also, you can color-code it and use an icon if you like. These features affect only the color and journal icon in the journals list. For example, in **Figure 9-17**, the Tips and Tricks journal is color-coded blue and has a small icon on it. After you've made your selections, click OK.

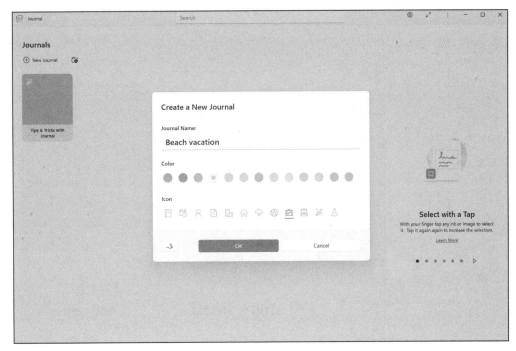

FIGURE 9-17

3. In the journal window you create, you can start writing. Use the toolbar at the bottom to configure pen and marker options. You can also click the plus sign (+) on the toolbar to insert a photo or a PDF, or you can click to open the computer's camera (shown in **Figure 9-18**).

4. On the left side of the screen, you can add more pages to your Journal, or you can switch from Page view to a Card view.

5. Journal entries are automatically saved. Just use the Back button on the toolbar to return to the main screen. Here, you can create new journals or open an existing journal.

Page view or Card view

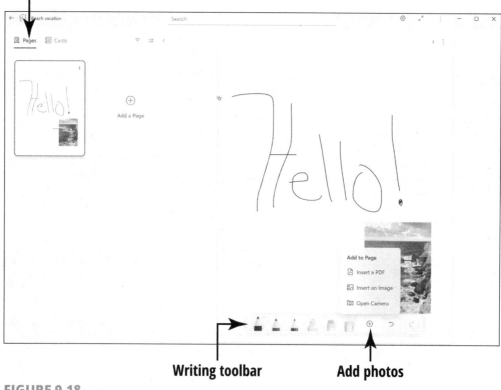

Writing toolbar   **Add photos**

FIGURE 9-18

3

Having Fun with Windows 11

Find and purchase apps at the Microsoft Store.

Take and edit photos and videos.

Play music and watch videos.

Chapter **10**

Exploring the Microsoft Store

You can do many things with Windows 11, such as send email, browse the web, play games, and look at photos and videos. You can read the news and chat with family and friends. All these functions and more involve computer programs. Back in the day, such programs were called *applications.* Now, we call them *apps.*

Windows 11 comes with a few apps installed, such as the Weather and Maps apps. (See Chapter 2 for information on using apps.) To obtain other apps — free or otherwise — you use the Microsoft Store.

To install an app from the Microsoft Store, you need a Microsoft account. See Chapter 4 for information on setting up a Microsoft account.

Microsoft tests and approves all apps in the Microsoft Store. For quality and security purposes, you can install Windows 11 apps only from the Microsoft Store.

In this chapter, you peruse the apps and games in the Microsoft Store, including those already installed on a new machine. You install a new game, discover how to manage the apps and games you own, and see how to rate and review an app or game. Finally, you find out how to make sure that the Microsoft Store can receive payments in case you want to buy an app or game.

Explore Apps and Games by Category

 1. Select the Microsoft Store icon on the taskbar. It looks like a shopping bag with the Windows 11 logo on it.

2. Look over the Store home screen, shown in **Figure 10-1**. The home screen shows top-rated apps and games, as well as apps and games that Microsoft thinks you will be interested in based on your previous purchases, if you made any. Notice the navigation bar along the left side of the screen (see **Figure 10-1**). It offers six choices: Home, Apps, Gaming, Arcade, Entertainment, and AI Hub. Wherever your travels take you in the Store, the navigation bar appears along the left side of the screen so that you can return to the home screen or redirect your search for apps, games, entertainment, and whatnot.

TIP

The Microsoft Store is, well . . . a store! Occasionally stores reorganize, and this is true for online stores as well. The good news is that you can typically figure out how to navigate and access different categories, even if Microsoft changes the look of things from time to time.

3. Select Apps on the navigation bar to go to the Apps screen.

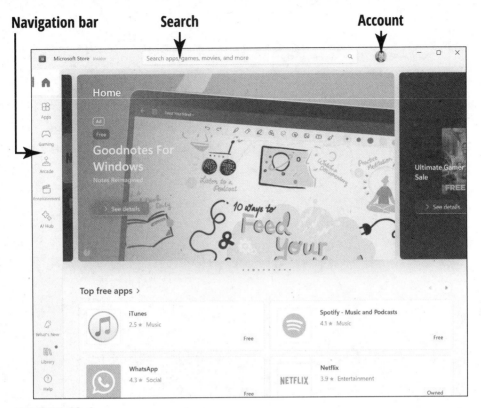

Navigation bar   **Search**   **Account**

FIGURE 10-1

4. If you scroll down this window, you see different app categories, such as Apps Specials, Best Selling, Productivity apps, and so forth. Locate the Top Free Apps heading, as shown in **Figure 10-2**. Click the heading to see a list of top free apps. After you click the heading, you see a Filters button option. You can select Filters to refine your search, as shown in **Figure 10-3**.

5. In the Top Free drop-down menu, select Top Free to see apps that you can install for free (see **Figure 10-3**). On the All Categories drop-down menu, select Education to see educational apps. You can experiment with different filter options to see what results you get.

Top free apps

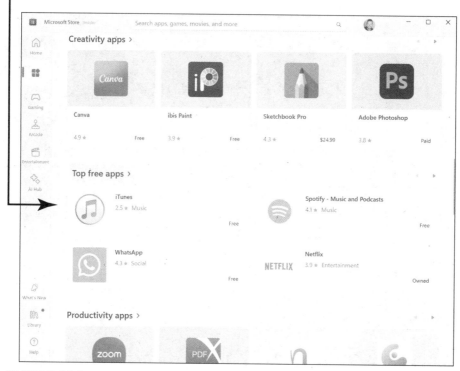

FIGURE 10-2

6. Select Gaming on the navigation bar and scroll down to see different gaming categories. You pass the familiar Best Selling and Top Free headings. You can select a heading to investigate all games in a category. The Gaming screen works just like the Apps screen.

7. Return to the Store home screen by selecting the Home button on the navigation bar.

Did you see an app or game you want to acquire as you completed these steps? If so, skip to "Install a New App or Game," later in this chapter.

TIP

Filter options

Filters button

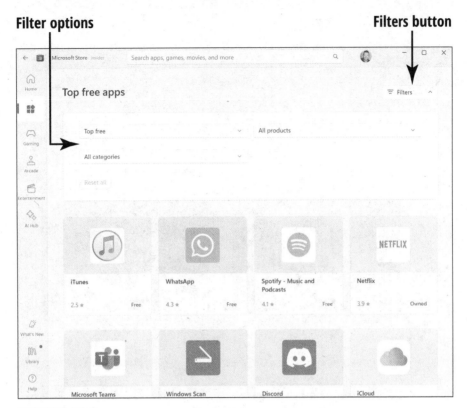

FIGURE 10-3

Search for an App or Game by Name

1. On any Store screen, click in the Search box. This box is at the top of the Microsoft Store window, as shown in **Figure 10-4**.

2. Type **chess** in the Search box and press Enter. As shown in **Figure 10-4**, games and apps with the word *chess* in their names appear in the Results screen. The Results screen tells you how many games and apps match your search. After this initial search, you can use the Filters feature to refine it if you like.

Search

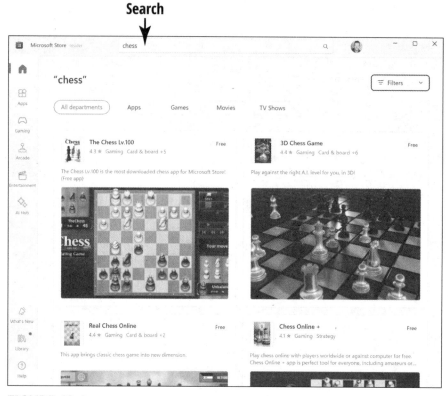

FIGURE 10-4

3. Select the Games button to see games with *chess* in their titles, as shown in **Figure 10-5**. After you select Games, you can select Filters to further refine your search if you like.

4. Proceed to the next section, "Install a New App or Game," or return to the home screen.

Games button

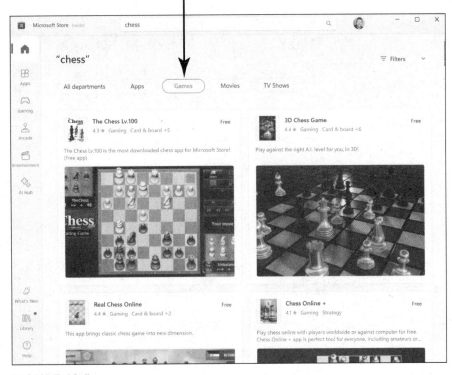

FIGURE 10-5

Install a New App or Game

1. In the Store, search for the Chess Free game. (See the earlier section "Search for an App or Game by Name" for details.) You'll see several free chess games in the search results, so just choose one and select it.

2. The screen shown in **Figure 10-6** appears. This (and any) game or app screen offers lots of information.

TIP

The Back button (left-pointing arrow) on the top left side of the screen takes you back to the previously viewed screen.

3. Notice that you see a description of the game as well as information about the number of ratings and the average. If you scroll down the page, you see more information about the game and ratings. You also see a Get button.

Ratings

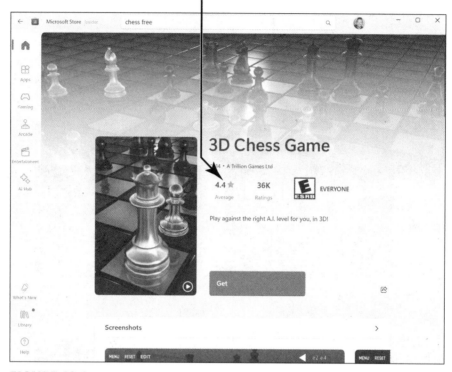

FIGURE 10-6

4. If you scroll down the page, note the section titled System Requirements. The Microsoft Store will automatically check your system to make sure that anything you download will work on your particular computer system (most of them should).

5. Select the Get button to download and install the free chess game.

6. If you're not already signed in, enter your Microsoft account email address and password on the screen that pops up. Then select Sign In.

Many apps are free. Before you buy an app, see the section "Add Billing Information to the Microsoft Store," later in this chapter.

TIP

If you purchase an app, you are buying a license to install that app on up to five machines using the same Microsoft account. The Microsoft Store will track how many times and on which machine the app is installed.

TIP

7. The download indicator appears and a progress bar shows the game being downloaded and installed.

TIP

Installing an app may take a few seconds or a few minutes. You can do anything while an app installs — except use the app.

8. To play the chess game or to use any game or app after you install it, enter the name of the app into the Search box on the Windows taskbar to find it, shown in **Figure 10-7**. Then, click the app's name in the search results to open it. Also note that the newly installed app may appear on the Start screen.

FIGURE 10-7

TIP

You can pin the chess game icon to the Start screen. See Chapter 3 for information on rearranging icons on the Start screen.

Examine Your Apps and Games

1. The Microsoft Store keeps track of which apps are installed on your Windows 11 computer. To see which apps and games you have, open the Microsoft Store and then select the Library icon on the navigation bar, as shown in **Figure 10-8**. On this screen, you can see all the apps that you have downloaded, and you see button options next to each, such as Launch, Manage, Open, and so forth.

2. Notice the category buttons available. By default, Apps is selected, but you can choose to see Games and Movies & TV (see **Figure 10-8**). Just select the button option you want.

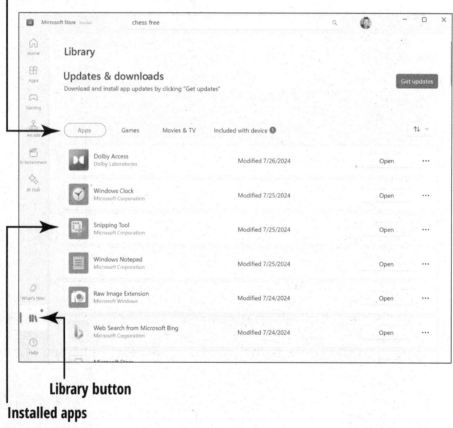

Category buttons

Library button

Installed apps

FIGURE 10-8

Rate and Review an App or Game

1. On the Library screen in the Microsoft Store (refer to **Figure 10-8**), select the free chess game you downloaded. If you don't have this game, see the section "Install a New App or Game," earlier in this chapter, or substitute any app or game you have installed.

2. In the Chess Free window, scroll down to the Ratings and Reviews category, shown in **Figure 10-9**. Select a star option to rate the game; then click the Write a Review button if you'd like to leave a review. The review screen appears (see **Figure 10-10**). Every app and game has an option to rate and review it if you've downloaded it.

You can rate or review only apps and games that you've installed, and you must be signed in to your Microsoft account.

TIP

3. In the review screen, choose the number of stars you want to give this game. (Select one star for the lowest rating; select five for the highest rating.)

FIGURE 10-9

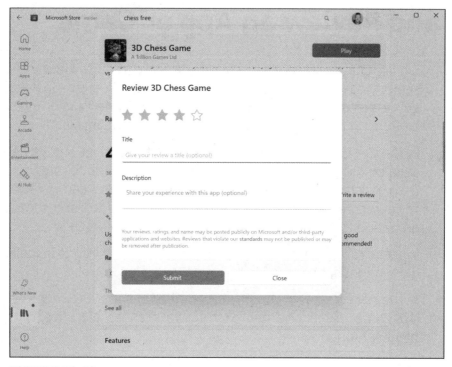

FIGURE 10-10

4. In the Description box, say what you will, up to 500 characters, including spaces and punctuation.

5. In the Title box, type a summary or overview of your comments, such as *Great app* or *Needs work*.

TIP

Your comments may help another person decide whether to install an app. In addition, the app's developer may use customer feedback to fix problems or add features.

TIP

Your Microsoft account name and picture (if you have one) appear with your review. Your email address will not appear.

6. Select the Submit button when you're done with your review.

Uninstalling an App

1. You may download an app, such as a game, and later decide you don't like or want the game any longer. You can easily uninstall anything you download from the Microsoft Store. First, search for the app you want to uninstall by entering its name in the Search box on the taskbar.

2. Select the app in the search results.

3. In the right pane of the search results, you see the option to Uninstall the app. Select the Uninstall option, as shown in **Figure 10-11**.

4. A dialog box appears, asking you to confirm. Select Uninstall again, and the app is uninstalled from your computer.

Uninstall

FIGURE 10-11

TIP

Available apps change often on the Microsoft Store. If you uninstall an app, there's no guarantee it will be available for download later. So, make sure you have no plans to use the app in the future before you uninstall.

Add Billing Information to the Microsoft Store

1. To add the billing information necessary to buy apps and games, select the Profile button next to the Search box. A pop-up menu appears with the option to select Payment Methods, as shown in **Figure 10-12**. Select this option, and a web page opens in Microsoft Edge.

TIP

See Chapter 4 for information on creating a Microsoft account.

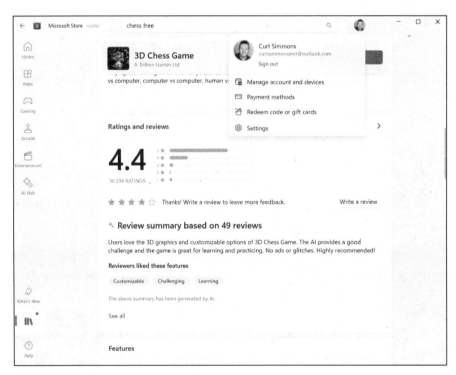

FIGURE 10-12

2. For security purposes, Microsoft asks you to enter your email address and password on the next screen. Enter your password and select the Sign In button.

3. Scroll through the screen to make sure that the information here is accurate. If you are not being billed to the correct credit card or you want to change the credit card to which you are billed, select Payment & Billing on the toolbar and choose Payment Options on the drop-down menu that appears.

4. Select a payment method (or select Payment Options if Microsoft already has your credit card information) and do the following:

   - Select your credit card type.

     You must fill out all parts of this form except for Address Line 2.

   - Enter your credit card number in the box provided. Don't enter dashes or spaces.

   - Under Expiration Date, select the month (MM) and year (YYYY) your card expires.

   - Enter your name as it appears on your credit card.

   - Under CVV, enter the three- or four-digit verification code from your credit card. (Select What's This? for an illustration of the location of this code on your card.)

5. In the Billing Address section, do the following:

   - Enter your street address, city, state, and ZIP code.

   - Select your Country/region.

   - Under Phone Number, enter your area code in the first box and the remainder of your number in the second box.

6. When you're ready to continue, select Save.

7. If any of your data is incomplete or invalid, the form remains onscreen. Look for indications of a problem. Review each entry before selecting Submit.

8. If your information was accepted, you return to the Your Account screen. Under Payment and billing info, note your credit card type, the last four digits of your number, and the expiration date.

TIP

Chapter **11**

Taking Photos and More

Windows 11 makes enjoying digital photos easy. You can pick and choose photos to look at or display a group of photos in a slide show. You can set a favorite photo to be your Lock screen background so that you see it every time you start Windows 11.

If you have a printer, you can print photos for yourself or to send them to someone by email. You can even make editing adjustments to your shots, or use AI to create an image from scratch. All these capabilities are built into your Windows 11 computer.

Of course, if you want to take your own photos, nothing beats having a digital camera or phone. Copy photos from your camera or phone to your Pictures folder for viewing and sharing. Or use the Camera app with the built-in camera found in many laptops and tablets.

In this chapter, you use the tools that come with Windows 11 for working with digital photos.

Take Photos (and Videos) with Your Computer

1. Select the Search box on the taskbar and type **camera**. Windows 11 will locate the Camera app for you. If you don't have a webcam, the app screen displays *We can't find your camera.* If you don't have a built-in webcam, or the resolution of the one you have is too low, you can easily add an external webcam. Simply plug the webcam into your computer — it's that easy.

TIP You can choose from many good webcam models. Generally, get the highest video resolution you can afford, because you'll probably use the camera for video chats. Consider the size of the camera, its attachment to your computer, and whether it has a microphone (you definitely need a microphone).

TIP For instructions about opening apps such as the Camera app, visit Chapter 2.

2. The first time you use the Camera app, you may see a screen that says *Let Windows camera access your location?* Select Yes to continue.

3. The Camera app opens, and there's a good chance you recognize the face staring back at you, such as the example in **Figure 11-1**. To take a photo, smile and then click or tap the Take Photo button (it's on the right side of the screen). You may notice a blue box dancing around your face as you get ready to take the photo (refer to **Figure 11-1**). This is a focusing box that the camera uses, but it won't actually show up in your photo. You may hear a shutter click when you take the shot. Your photo is placed automatically in a folder called Camera Roll in the Pictures folder.

TIP Select the Camera Roll icon in the lower-right corner of the Camera app to view the photo you most recently took. After that, you can select See All Photos to open the Photos App and view photos there. (Select the Back button in the upper-left corner of the screen to resume taking photos.)

4. To take a time-lapse photo, use the Photo Timer button on the left side of the screen. Select this button one, two, or three times to tell the Camera app to wait 2, 5, or 10 seconds before taking the photo. Then click or tap the Camera button and wait 2, 5, or 10 seconds for the photo to be taken.

Settings   **Focusing box**   **Take a photo**
Take a video

Timer   **Camera roll**
Scan a barcode

FIGURE 11-1

5. Select the Video button (refer to **Figure 11-1**). Nothing happens until you click or tap the Video button a second time, at which point you're in moving pictures. A counter indicates the length of the video. Short is sweet in video. You can speak, too. Click or tap the Video button to stop the video. As with photos you take with the Camera app, videos are saved initially in the Camera Roll subfolder of the Pictures folder. Select the Camera button to turn off the video function and return to taking still photos (with the next click or tap).

Leave the Camera app open to explore the Camera settings, which I explain next.

Choose Camera Settings

1. If the Camera app isn't open, open it now. Then select the Settings button located in the upper-left corner of the Camera window (refer to **Figure 11-1**). The Settings panel opens, as shown in **Figure 11-2** and **Figure 11-3**. From here, you can tell the Camera app how to take photos and videos.

TIP

Depending on the size of your screen, you may need to scroll down to see all of the Settings panel. Just move your mouse over the panel, and a scroll bar appears on the right side.

2. Select the On button for Show Advanced Controls for Photos and Videos. This action turns on Windows Studio Effects. You see a button on the camera app in the upper-right corner when you choose to take a video. When you select the Video button, a drop-down menu appears from which you can choose some helpful settings, such as automatic framing, portrait light, eye contact, and so forth, as shown in **Figure 11-4**).

FIGURE 11-2

FIGURE 11-3

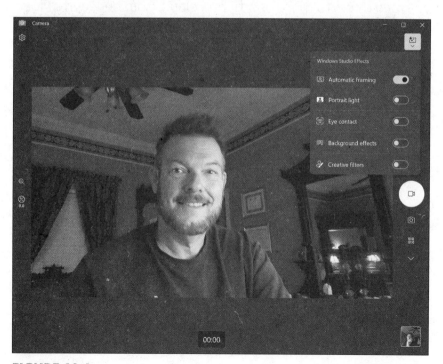

FIGURE 11-4

3. Choose a Framing Grid option to help aim the camera. For example, the Crosshairs option places crossing lines in the center of the screen so that you know where the center of your photos will be.

4. Under Photos, decide how you want to take photos:

   - **Photo Quality:** These options determine the aspect ratio and the size of photos in pixels. For example, you can shoot narrow (the 4:3 options) or widescreen (the 16:9 options) photos.

   - **Time Lapse:** Choose this option when you want to take a series of time-lapse photos (the previous topic in this chapter explains how to take a time-lapse photo). For example, with this option selected and the Photo Timer set to 2 seconds, the Camera app takes a time-lapse photo every 2 seconds until you click or tap the Camera button a second time, which tells the app to stop taking photos.

5. Under Videos, decide how you want to take videos:

   - **Video Quality:** These options determine the aspect ratio and the number of pixels that appear in video frames. Notice that the fps (frames per second) setting in each option is the same, 30. *Aspect ratio* refers to the proportional relationship between a video's width and height. The most common aspect ratios are 16:9 (widescreen) and 4:3 (old-fashioned TV). A *pixel* is one point of color. Suffice it to say, the more pixels in the setting, the clearer the video is.

   - **Flicker reduction:** These options reduce the flickering that can occur when the video is taken under fluorescent light. The 50 Hz (hertz) setting applies to the U.S. and Canada, where the AC (alternating electrical current) runs at 50 Hz; the 60 Hz setting applies to the rest of the world.

6. Return to the Camera app by clicking or tapping the Camera app screen.

7. Return to the Start screen. See the section "View Photos with the Photos App" to see and maybe edit the photos you just took.

Copy Photos from Your Camera

1. If your digital camera came with a cable, connect that cable to the camera, connect the other end of the cable to a USB port on your computer, and turn on your camera. If your laptop or tablet has a built-in card slot, you can take the memory card out of the camera and insert it in that slot.

2. If your computer doesn't have a built-in card slot, consider buying a small memory card reader that plugs into your computer and works with your camera's memory card. You don't need a multicard reader, just a reader with a single slot the size of your camera card. I consider a card reader to be more convenient than using a cable.

The techniques described here for importing photos from a camera also apply to videos. Follow these steps as well to copy videos from your digital camera to your computer.

3. Windows 11 detects your camera and may briefly display a notification indicating *Select to choose what happens with this device.* Select Open Device to View Files, if that option is available, open File Explorer to the photos on your camera, as shown in **Figure 11-5**. Then skip to Step 4. If you didn't catch the notification in time or you didn't see the notification, continue to Step 4 to import photos another way.

See Chapter 3 for information on increasing the time a notification remains onscreen.

4. Select the File Explorer icon on the taskbar to start File Explorer. Then look for and select your camera in the navigation pane on the left side of the screen (refer to **Figure 11-5**). Your camera is located under *This PC* in the navigation pane.

See Chapter 15 for detailed information about using File Explorer.

5. In File Explorer, select the photos you want to copy from your camera to your computer. Depending on your camera setup, the photos may be in a subfolder (refer to **Figure 11-5**). Use these techniques to select the photos:

   - Hold down the Ctrl button and click or tap photos to select them individually.

   - Press Ctrl+A to select all the photos in a folder.

Select your camera or one of its subfolders

FIGURE 11-5

6. Copy the photos you selected so that you can paste them into a folder on your computer. Use one of these techniques to copy the photos:

   - Press Ctrl+C.

   - On the toolbar in File Explorer, select the Copy button.

7. In File Explorer, select the folder where you want to copy your photos.

TIP

If you want to be able to view and edit your photos with the Photos app, select the Pictures folder or one of its subfolders and copy the photos there.

TIP

Organizing photos can be a challenge. If you dump more than a few dozen photos into the Pictures folder without using folders, finding a specific photo later will be difficult. Using folders with unintelligible names doesn't help, either. I base most of my folder names on the year and month (such as 2021–06) or the subject or location where I took the photos. You can name your folders whatever you want, but choose names that are meaningful to you and will help you find specific photos later.

8. Paste the photos into the folder you selected in Step 7. Use one of these techniques:

- Press Ctrl+V.

- On the toolbar in File Explorer, select the Paste button.

TIP

If you often import photos from a digital camera or memory card, you can speed the process by telling Windows to open File Explorer immediately when you attach your camera or memory card to your computer. Select the Search icon on the taskbar and type **autoplay settings**; then select that option when it appears in your search. The AutoPlay window opens, as shown in **Figure 11-6**. In the Memory Card and Camera sections, choose Open Folder (or Open Device) to View Files (File Explorer).

FIGURE 11-6

TIP

Do you need to get photos from your phone to your Windows 11 computer? Check your phone's documentation for details. Different phone makes and models work differently in how you connect the phone to a computer. You may also be able to connect your phone to your computer with a cable or with Windows Phone Link (see Chapter 1), or you may access your phone's photos in the cloud or even email them to yourself.

View Photos with the Photos App

1. The Photos app, which is built into Windows 11, is a robust app for viewing and editing photos on your PC. To open the Photos app, select the Search box on the taskbar and type **photos** in the Search box; then select the Photos app in the search results. The Photos screen opens to the Gallery window, as shown in **Figure 11-7**. It can show you the photos on your computer or even your camera (if it's connected to the computer).

2. If you don't see any pictures, go to one of these earlier sections:

   - If you have a digital camera, see "Copy Photos from Your Camera."

   - If your computer has a built-in camera or a webcam, see "Take Photos (and Videos) with Your Computer."

3. If you see pictures, either scroll down or drag the timeline on the right side of the screen to see more photos. Photos are presented by the dates on which they were taken. You can also navigate to different locations to select photos using the options on the left toolbar, such as your computer, iCloud photos, or even a connected camera.

TIP

You can take a screenshot — a picture of the current screen — by pressing ⌘+Print Screen. (A touchscreen or mouse equivalent is not available.) The screen dims slightly to indicate the capture, which is stored automatically in the Screenshots folder in your Pictures folder. Use this technique to create your own documentation of problems or something you want to see again later.

4. Select the Gallery Types and Sizes button on the top tool to choose different sizes and layouts for viewing your photos in the Photos app (refer to **Figure 11-7**). Use them to examine and locate photos.

Select a location of the photos you want to see   **Gallery Types and Sizes**

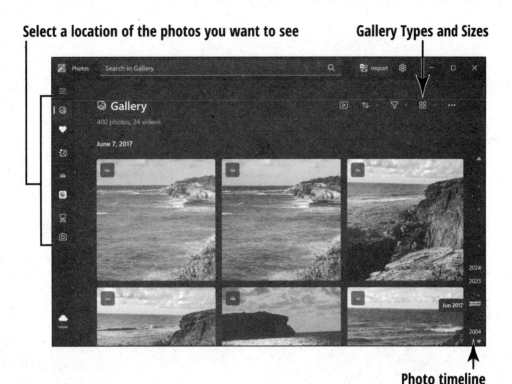

Photo timeline

FIGURE 11-7

5. Double-click any photo to display it full size in the Photos app window, as shown in **Figure 11-8**. This action opens a new window displaying the photo. When looking at a single photo, you can scroll from photo to photo by selecting the Previous or Next button or by clicking or tapping the right edge or left edge of the screen. You can also press the PageDown key (forward) or PageUp key (back). Note that the Previous and Next buttons don't appear until you hover or touch the right or left sides of the window.

6. Select the Slideshow button on the toolbar (refer to **Figure 11-8**). The photos appear in succession. Stop the slide show by clicking or tapping a photo.

7. Zoom in and out on a photo using one of these methods (repeat to zoom in or out more):

    • **Mouse:** Click the Zoom In or Zoom Out buttons at the bottom right to zoom in or out on your photo.

- **Touchscreen:** Touch two fingers on the screen. Move your fingers apart to zoom in. Pinch your fingers closer together to zoom out.

- **Keyboard:** Press Ctrl+plus sign (actually, press the equal sign — no need to press the Shift key) to zoom in. Press Ctrl+minus sign to zoom out.

TIP

Zoom in to see part of a photo made larger.

Use the Delete button in the toolbar to delete a photo. (See Chapter 15 for information on undeleting files.)

8. Select the arrow on the left side of the toolbar to return to your photo collection. In this view, you can see more than one photo.

FIGURE 11-8

TIP

To return to the main Photos app window, click the Close button (refer to **Figure 11-8**).

Edit Photos Using the Photos App

1. You can use the Photos app to make some editing changes to a photo. In the Photos app, double-click the photo you want to edit. This action opens a new window. Then select the Edit button located at the upper right of the window. The Editing window opens, as shown in **Figure 11-9**. This window offers many tools for touching up photos. To edit a photo, select any of the following tools from the toolbar at the top of the window (refer to **Figure 11-9**): The following steps tell you what you can do with each tool.

FIGURE 11-9

2. Many photos can be improved by *cropping,* which involves cutting out distracting elements and keeping just part of the photo. You might crop a photo to concentrate on its most important part. Select the Free button under the photo; then select an aspect ratio or choose the Custom aspect ratio and drag the size or corners of the picture box until the photo is to your liking. The box tells you which parts will remain after cropping, as shown in **Figure 11-10**.

FIGURE 11-10

TIP

Sometimes when you import photos from a digital camera or scanner, they arrive askew because the photographer turned the camera the wrong way when shooting. You can correct this error by selecting Crop & Rotate and then selecting the Rotate button until the photo turns right-side-up.

3. Select the Adjustment button to access a collection of slider bars to adjust the overall exposure of a photo. Use the slider bars to adjust the brightness, exposure, contrast, highlights, shadows, and vignette effect. Experiment with these options to see how they impact the overall look of your photo.

4. Select the Filter button to choose a color filter for your photo. If you select the Auto Enhance option, the Photos app tries to improve the overall color of your photo, or you can choose a specific filter, such as Punch, Golden, Radiate, Warm Contrast, and so forth. Select the filter you want and it's automatically applied to the image. Don't like what you see? Select the Undo button, shown in **Figure 11-11**. Selecting this button restores a photograph to its original, pristine state.

Undo   **Select a filter option**

FIGURE 11-11

5. Select Markup to add freehand notes or highlighting to an image. At the bottom of the image, you see two pen options and highlighter. Select the desired markup tool and add anything you want to your photo. Use the Remove Markup button to remove any marks you don't want to keep.

6. Select Erase to remove background items you don't want in your image. Select a brush size using the slider bar and click the object in the image you want to remove. The Photos app will attempt to remove the object and replace it with more of the surrounding background.

7. Select Background to remove or blur the entire background of a photo. You have only three options here: Blur, Remove, or Replace. You can use Replace to change the background to another color. This tool works especially well if you have a close-up of a subject, such as a person, but a distracting background. You can simply blur or remove the background to improve the photo.

8. Select the Restyle option, which uses the power of AI to restyle you photo using a built-in theme, such as fantasy, anime, or surrealism. Also, you can describe the style you would like in the Describe What Style You'd Like to apply response box. For example, in **Figure 11-12**, I've asked AI to make the ocean scene more dramatic. AI will attempt to create the style you want. You may or may not like the results, so use the Undo button on the toolbar if you want to try a different style.

9. When you're done editing your photo, select the Save Options button on the right side of the toolbar and choose Save a Copy. This action keeps your original photo untouched while saving a new copy of your edited photo.

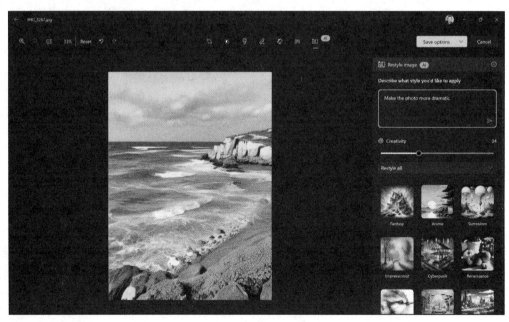

FIGURE 11-12

Print Photos Using the Photos App

1. If necessary, connect the cable from your printer to the USB port on your computer and make sure that your printer is turned on.

2. In the Photos app, double-click the photo you want to print. This action opens the photo in a new window

3. Select the Print button on the left side of the toolbar (it looks like a printer). The Print window appears, as shown in **Figure 11-13**.

   Here's a handy keyboard shortcut that works in any app: Press Ctrl+P to open the Print window straightaway.

TIP

4. Select a printer. Note the preview. Select the Print button.

FIGURE 11-13

Chapter 14 explains printing in detail.

TIP

Create an Image with AI

1. Open the Photos app. On the left toolbar, choose Image Creator.

2. In the Image Creator window, you can choose a category, such as baking ideas, wallpaper, or something else. Or you can simply ask AI to create anything you want. For example, in **Figure 11-14**, I ask for **winter woods**. After you finish typing, select the Generate button.

3. Image Creator creates several images for you to choose from. If the images aren't quite right, try adding more detail to your creation prompt. For example, I type **scary winter woods** and select Generate again. Image Creator then generates a new set of images for me to explore.

4. After you find an image you like, select it. Two button options appear on the bottom left of the image. You can choose to generate variations of the image, or you can choose to save it, as shown in **Figure 11-15**.

TIP

Image Creator is a fun way to create images for all sorts of needs. For example, say you're hosting a birthday party for a child. For that party, you need an image of a cat wearing a cowboy hat, as shown in **Figure 11-16**. No problem! Just ask Image Creator to make it for you, and then save the image to use as needed!

FIGURE 11-14

Select the photo you like

Choose to create variations or save the photo

FIGURE 11-15

FIGURE 11-16

Chapter **12**

Enjoying Music and Videos

The term *media* on computers refers to something other than text. Audio and video are examples of media. *Audio* is a catchall term for music and other sound files, such as books on CD. *Video* includes files that you can shoot with your digital camera as well as Hollywood blockbusters.

The delivery of music has come a long way from Edison's wax cylinder or even vinyl LPs. Nowadays, music is almost entirely digital (although vinyl has been making a comeback in some circles). Although Windows 11 doesn't provide music or movies, you can easily listen to and play them using built-in software, or you can download other apps as well. With Windows 11, you can stream music or videos from a service provider, which sends music and videos over the internet to your computer. You can also listen to and watch downloaded media that exists on your computer.

In this chapter, you download apps to access different music and movie services to which you can subscribe (or may already be subscribed). You can also listen to an audio file or watch any video file using Media Player — an old piece of software that's been revamped in Windows 11. You can make an audio recording, and edit and create videos using Clipchamp, which is software built into Windows 11.

Download Music and Movie Apps

1. Select the Microsoft Store icon on the taskbar to open the Microsoft Store. See Chapter 10 for more information about using the Microsoft Store.

2. In the Store, search for any music or movie app you want. Windows 11 doesn't provide music or movie subscriptions, but you can download apps for subscriptions you want or may already have. For example, maybe you use Apple Music on your iPhone, or maybe you watch movies on your TV using Netflix or Amazon Prime. You can download these apps from the Microsoft Store to Windows 11 so that way you can access those services on your computer. For example, say you have a Netflix account. If you search Netflix on the Microsoft Store, you see the app that you can install on your Windows 11 computer, as shown in **Figure 12-1**. Click Install to install the app of your choice.

3. After you install an app, you can access it using the Search box on the taskbar. Just search for the app's name. For example, in **Figure 12-2**, you see that the iTunes app has been installed from the Store and is now accessible as an app on Windows 11.

TIP

You can pin any app you use frequently to the taskbar or Start menu. See Chapter 2 for more information about pinning apps.

4. After you open the app you downloaded, the app prompts you to log in to your account.

TIP

Don't have an account? Most apps give you the option to create a new account, choose a subscription plan, set up payment options, and so on. You can also check out subscription options by visiting the provider's website. For example, if you're interested in using Hulu to watch movies, just visit www.hulu.com to get subscription details.

TIP

Not sure which music or movie streaming service is right for you? Try asking Copilot AI for some suggestions, as well as website addresses to check out. See Chapter 2 for more information about using Copilot AI.

FIGURE 12-1

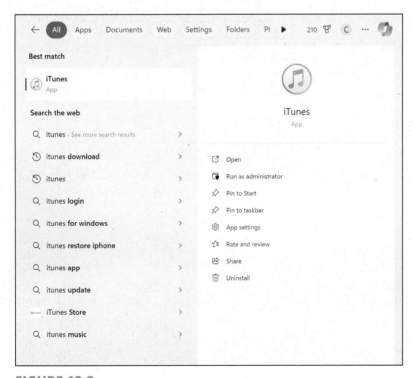

FIGURE 12-2

Open Audio and Video Files with Media Player

1. Double-click an audio or video file stored on your PC.

TIP

By default, the Music and Video folders you find in File Explorer hold audio and video files. However, you can store audio and video files in any folder you want. Maybe you have some vacation videos taken with your phone, camera, or even drone. You can store those files on Windows 11 in any desired folder. See Chapter 15 for more information about files and folders.

TIP

Music and movies you access from a service such as Spotify, iTunes, Disney+, and others aren't stored locally on your PC. You can access those files only by using the service provider's website or the service provider's app.

2. Windows may ask you what program you want to use to open the audio or video file. Choose Media Player, shown in **Figure 12-3**. Select Always or Just Once to tell Windows whether you always want to open this kind of file with Media Player, or just this one time.

FIGURE 12-3

3. The file now opens in Media Player. Media Player is a basic playback app, shown in **Figure 12-4**. The toolbar on the bottom gives you the following playback controls:

- **Shuffle:** If you're playing through numerous files in the same folder, the shuffle option allows Media Player to randomly choose which file plays next.

- **Previous:** Plays the previous file in a folder of audio or video files.

- **Skip Back:** This button moves the file playback 10 seconds backward.

- **Play/Pause:** Press to play the audio or video file. When the file is playing, this button turns to a Pause button. Press to pause playback.

- **Skip Forward:** This button moves the file playback 10 seconds forward.

- **Next:** This button plays the next file in the selected folder.

- **Repeat:** Press this button to play the media file over and over until you press Pause

- **Languages and subtitles:** For video files with audio options, you can use this menu to choose languages and to display subtitles, if available.

- **Volume:** Select this button to manage the volume.

- **Full Screen:** Select this button to view a video full screen on your computer. Select the button again to exit full screen (or press ESC on your keyboard).

- **Mini Player:** Select this button to make Media Player convert to a mini player, which is a small version of Media Player. This feature is helpful when you want to use Media Player, but you don't want it to take up a lot of space on your screen.

- **More Options:** Select this button to access a menu for additional options, such as casting a video to another device (which makes the video play on another device, such as a TV), accessing an audio equalizer, adjusting video playback speed, and so on.

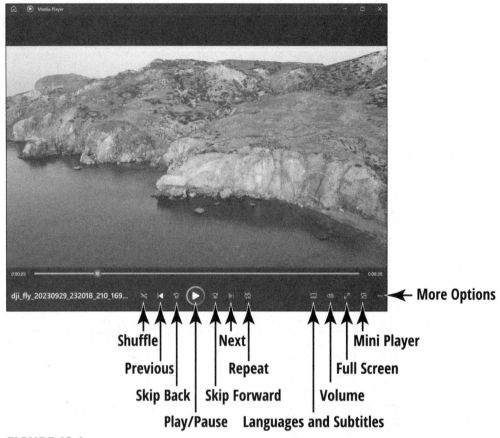

← More Options

Shuffle
Previous
Next
Repeat
Skip Back | Skip Forward
Volume
Mini Player
Full Screen
Play/Pause   Languages and Subtitles

FIGURE 12-4

Navigate Files with Media Player

1. In the Search box on the taskbar, search for Media Player and open it from the search results.

2. Media Player opens to the home screen, which shows you any media you've recently watched or listened to. Click any file here to watch or listen to it again.

3. On the left side of Media Player, you see a toolbar with a few different navigation options, shown in **Figure 12-5**:

   - **Search:** Select this button to search for any media file by name.

   - **Home:** Media Player opens here by default and shows you recent media you've accessed.

- **Music library:** This button opens the Music folder on your PC and shows you any audio files stored there.

- **Video Library:** This button opens the Videos folder on your PC and shows you any video files stored there.

- **Play Queue:** Select this button to organize a list of your audio or video files so that they play in a certain order.

- **Play List:** Select this button to create a playlist of media items. For example, you can organize a series of songs to play in a certain order.

Music Library

Home

Search

Play List

Play Queue

Video Library

FIGURE 12-5

You can also select Open Navigation on the toolbar to see an expanded version of the icon options.

TIP

Adjust Media Player Settings

1. Select the Search box on the taskbar and search for Media Player. Select Media Player in the search results to open it. On the left toolbar, select the Setting icon toward the bottom. Media Player is a basic app that doesn't give you a lot of Settings options to choose from, but you may want to make adjustments to the Libraries options, shown in **Figure 12-6**. Use the Video screen to watch videos.

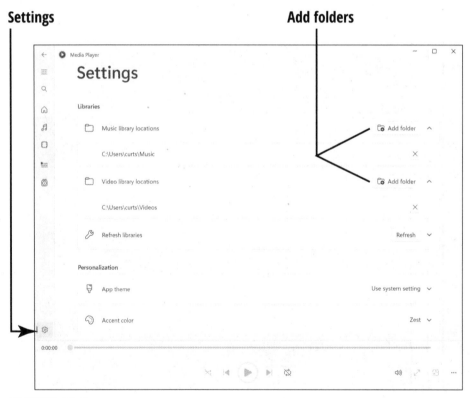

FIGURE 12-6

2. By default, Media Player looks in the C:\Users*Your Name*\Music and C:\Users*Your Name*\Videos folders. However, you may have media stored in other folders as well. For example, maybe you have numerous videos from a recent trip in a specific folder called Trip. To tell Media Player to also access your Trip folder, click Add folder. Then you can select the Trip folder as well as any other folders where media may be stored. You can also add specific folders for music.

Make a Sound Recording

1. Open the Sound Recorder app to record your voice or any other sounds you want. In the Search box on the taskbar, type **Sound Recorder** and open the app from the results window.

TIP It probably goes without saying, but your computer needs a built-in microphone or microphone jack for plugging in a microphone if you want to make voice recordings.

TIP The first time you run Sound Recorder, a dialog box may appear, asking "Let Sound Recorder access your documents library?" Select Yes. To change this setting later, go to the Settings app. You also may need to give the app permission to use your computer's microphone. If so, a message will appear asking for permission

2. Select the Record button (or press Ctrl+R) to begin a recording. A timer tells you how long your recording is. You can select the Pause/Resume Recording button to temporarily stop a recording. Select the Pause/Resume Recording button again to continue recording, as shown in **Figure 12-7**.

3. Select the Stop Recording button (located on the bottom toolbar) to end a recording. The name of your recording appears in the list under the generic name *Recording*. To give it a more descriptive name, right-click or tap to display the recording's context menu (shown in **Figure 12-8**), choose Rename, enter a name, and select the Rename button.

TIP To delete a recording, display its context menu and choose Delete.

FIGURE 12-7

FIGURE 12-8

TIP

To access a Sound Recorder file, perhaps to copy or move it, display its context menu (refer to **Figure 12-15**) and choose Show in Folder. The Sound Recordings folder opens. From here, you can copy or move the file. See Chapter 15 if you need instructions for handling files.

Create a Video with AI

Phones, cameras, drones — all kinds of devices record video these days. Perhaps you have a bunch of video clips from a vacation, a grandkid's birthday party, or some other event you don't want to forget. Wouldn't it be great if you could easily make one video instead of having a bunch of random files? Well, you can! Clipchamp is a video editor app included with Windows 11. Because it's built in, it's free to use (although some features require a subscription). Clipchamp has several different features that you can explore, but the most important is assembling video clips into one video. You can do this task with the help of AI or from scratch.

1. Type **Clipchamp** into the Search box on the taskbar and then choose the app in the results. Clipchamp opens and you see a few different options. Select the Create a Video with AI option in the main window, as shown in **Figure 12-9**.

2. Give the video a title and then click to add your media to the project. You can add as many different video files as you like. The thumbnails for each video appear in the media window, as shown in **Figure 12-10**. When you're done adding media, select Get Started.

3. In the Style window that appears, choose a style option you like and click Next.

4. In the Length window, choose Landscape or Portrait and about how long you want the video to be. Clipchamp AI will edit your video to fit within the timeframe you want. Note that you can also choose Full Length so that none of the clips are edited. When you're done, select Next.

FIGURE 12-9

Add Media

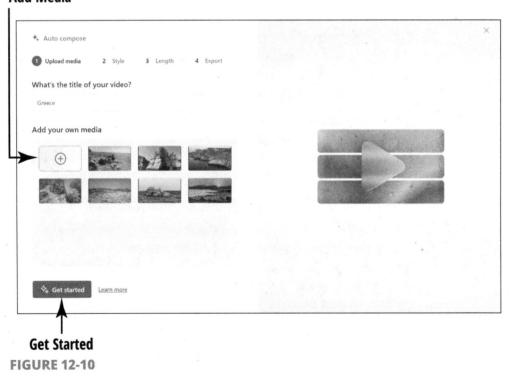

Get Started

FIGURE 12-10

5. Clipchamp creates your video. In the Export window, you can watch the video to see whether you like it. If so, click Export to save it. If not, you can have AI create a new version or adjust the music selection, or you can choose to take over the project and edit it in the timeline, shown in **Figure 12-11**. See the next section to find out more about timeline editing.

FIGURE 12-11

TIP

AI makes a lot of guesses about what you might want. It's not unusual to have AI create several versions before you find one you like. Also, the AI option is good for simple videos. If you need clips to flow in a certain order or you want to trim away specific portions of video that you don't want, starting from scratch is best.

Create a Video from Scratch

1. Open Clipchamp and choose to create a video from scratch.
2. Click the Import Media button and select the video files you want to include in the project (see **Figure 12-12**).

3. After you've imported the media you want to use, drag the clips onto the timeline in the order you want (see **Figure 12-12**).

4. When the clips are in order, select the Export button to finalize and export the video file. Of course, before doing so, you may want to make other changes. Read on!

Import Media   **Export**

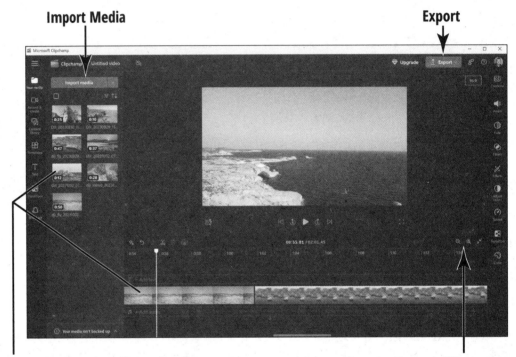

Drag imported media to timeline   **Zoom In/Zoom Out**
FIGURE 12-12

 To change the order of clips on the timeline, just drag a clip to a new timeline location.

TIP

 Use the Zoom In/Zoom Out buttons on the timeline to make the clips easier to see and manage.

TIP

Split or Trim a Clip

TIP

1. When you work with video clips, you may need to split one into a few different pieces so that you can organize the clips or move them around the timeline. You may also need to trim a clip, which means that you remove a portion of the beginning or ending of the clip.

   Splitting and trimming gives you a simple way to work with your video clips so that you keep only the portions you want and in the order you want.

2. To split a clip, place the playhead where you want to split the clip on the timeline. Then select the Split button, shown in **Figure 12-13**.

Split   **Place the playhead where you want to split the clip**

FIGURE 12-13

3. To trim a clip, position the mouse at the beginning or end of a clip. Then hold down the left mouse key and drag. This action trims away the portions of the clip you no longer want to keep, as shown in **Figure 12-14**.

TIP

If you make a mistake, just drag the clip back to its previous position and Clipchamp restores the video.

Drag the edge of a clip to trim

FIGURE 12-14

Add Transitions and Text

1. Add transitions to video clips so that they smoothly transition from one clip to the next. On the Clipchamp toolbar, select Transitions.

2. Choose a transition and drag it between two clips on the timeline. Click Play to preview the transition. Don't like it? Select Undo to remove the transition (see **Figure 12-15**).

3. Repeat these steps to add transitions between other clips.

TIP

Although you can use a different transition between each clip if you like, videos tend to look better when you use the same transition throughout. You want the transitions to help your video clips look good when moving from one scene to the next, but you don't want transitions to become the star of the show.

4. To add text to a clip, position the playhead where you want to add the text. Then select Text on the left toolbar.

Select Transitions   **Undo**

Drag a transition to the timeline between two clips   **Play**

FIGURE 12-15

5. Choose a text style and drag the text style to the timeline where you want the text to appear.

6. On the right side of the Clipchamp interface, you can input your text and make adjustments to font, colors, and other features, depending on the text style you chose (see **Figure 12-16**).

Anytime you're ready, click Export to save and export your video.

TIP

Clipchamp offers many additional features, such as to add music and narration and to use templates and numerous effects. You can find more about using Clipchamp and watch tutorials at https:// clipchamp.com/en/training-center/.

Select text

Add your text and make adjustments

Drag a text style to the timeline

FIGURE 12-16

4

Beyond the Basics

Chapter **13**

Maintaining Windows 11

W indows 11 is a bit like a car. To make it run well, you have to maintain it.

Windows 11 uses several tools to keep you informed of issues that pertain to your computer's health. The Reliability Monitor can help you pinpoint problems with hardware and software.

Many machines, such as coffee makers, do the same basic tasks over and over. Your computer, however, can be programmed to do something it's never done before. To make your computer capable of doing new things, you install new programs. On the other hand, your computer may have some programs that you'll never use and wouldn't miss. You don't have to get rid of them, but doing so is easy enough and can make your computer run better.

In this chapter, you work with the Windows Security screen to check your computer's health status. You also install a program and, optionally, uninstall one. This chapter also shows how to make your computer work faster by controlling the startup apps, defragmenting your hard drive, and deleting unnecessary system files. Finally, you discover how to protect your computer against spyware, viruses, and other foreign invaders.

Install a New Program or App

1. You can install software that you download from the web. (Windows 11 apps must be installed through the Microsoft Store.) In this set of steps, you install Audacity, a free program for editing audio files. To install Audacity, open the Edge browser and enter `audacityteam.org/download` in the address bar. You land on the web page for downloading Audacity Muse, an app. (See Chapter 6 for information on using the Edge browser.)

TIP

If a website offers to install a program automatically, regard that suggestion with suspicion. It may be legitimate or it may be malevolent. Decline downloads from sources that you don't know and trust already.

2. Select the Audacity Installer link for Windows to go to the web page for downloading programs.

3. Select the Audacity Installer link to start the download; however, note that Edge may do this for you automatically. Either way, a Downloads pop-up menu appears, showing that the software has been downloaded. Choose Open File on this pop-up, shown in **Figure 13-1**.

4. The User Account Control dialog box appears. Select the Yes button to tell Windows you want to download and install the program. In the Select Setup Language dialog box, choose English and select OK.

TIP

Generally, if the installer for a program offers Express or Custom installation options, choose the Express option to let the installer set up the program without further input from you. The Custom or Advanced Settings option allows you to specify where to install the program and, perhaps, which parts of the program to install.

5. The software installs on your computer. Should you see any additional dialog boxes asking you to continue the installation, click Next. The Audacity program opens on your desktop when installation is complete.

Download link

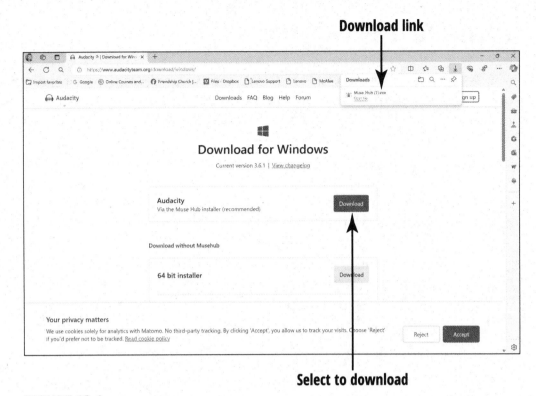

Select to download

FIGURE 13-1

TIP

Many programs or apps try to connect to the internet for updates during installation or when you run the installed program. The first time you run a program, you may be asked whether you want to register the program or configure some aspect of the program. Go with the default (assumed) responses if you're not sure.

6. Close Audacity. You can do that by selecting the Close button (the X) in the upper-right corner of the screen.

TIP

In the unlikely event that you need to install a program that comes on a CD or DVD, insert the program disc into your computer's disc drive or tray, label side up (or, if your computer has a vertical disc slot, insert the disc with the label side facing left). The AutoPlay dialog box appears. Select the option to run Install or Setup. User Account Control may ask whether you really want to run this program. (Windows 11 tries to keep you from installing software unintentionally by asking for confirmation.)

Remove a Program

1. Unlike Windows 11 apps from the Microsoft Store, you install other programs from a website. However, some of those programs may be considered apps. You uninstall programs and apps differently on Windows 11. To see which programs are installed, open the Control Panel. Select the Search box on the taskbar and type **control panel**; then select Control Panel in the Search results.

TIP

Many of the functions covered in this chapter are part of the Control Panel, which presents many functions for tweaking your computer setup.

2. In the Control Panel window (shown in **Figure 13-2**), under Programs, select Uninstall a Program. (You don't have to uninstall anything right now; you can simply see what the option offers.) You see the Programs and Features window.

3. The Programs and Features window lists programs installed on Windows 11, but it does not list your Windows 11 apps. Initially, these programs are sorted by name. You may want to see the date you last used each program, because a program you haven't used in ages may be a candidate for removal. (Otherwise, skip to Step 5.) Use one of the following techniques to display the date last used:

   - **Mouse:** Move the mouse pointer over any column heading, such as Name. Click the right mouse button.

   - **Touchscreen:** Tap and hold down on any column heading, such as Name. When a box appears around your fingertip, lift your finger.

4. On the context menu that appears, select More. In the Choose Details window (shown in **Figure 13-3**), select Last Used On and then select the OK button. The Last Used On column appears to the right of all the other columns.

TIP

Before you uninstall a program that you may want to reinstall later, make sure you have access to the installer file. This file may be on a CD or DVD, for older programs, or you may need to know where to download it from the web again. You have no undo option when you uninstall a program.

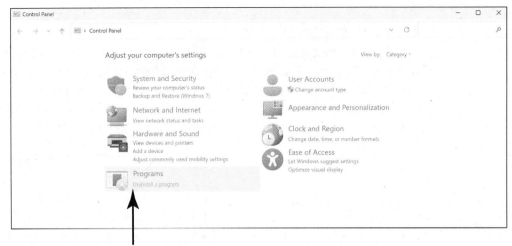

Uninstall a program

FIGURE 13-2

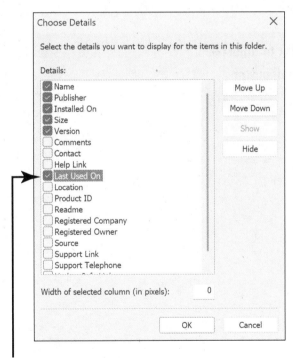

Last Used On

FIGURE 13-3

5. To uninstall a program, select it

6. Select the Uninstall button (located above the list of program names), shown in **Figure 13-4**. Some programs offer the Change and Repair options as well as Uninstall. Repair or Change may be useful for a program that you want to keep but isn't running as expected. When Windows 11 asks whether you really to uninstall, select Yes or No.

7. If you uninstalled a program, it will no longer appear in the Programs and Features window.

TIP

Just because you can uninstall a program doesn't mean you should. You can simply ignore programs you don't use. Look at a program's name, publisher, and date installed to determine whether you actually use a program. You may recognize a program you installed recently, as opposed to one installed before you got your computer. If you find that it's more productive to remove large programs than small ones, repeat Steps 3 and 4 to group by size.

Select the program you want to uninstall

Select the Uninstall button

![Programs and Features window screenshot showing a list of installed programs. Highlighted row: Lenovo Vantage Service, Lenovo Group Ltd., 7/31/2024, 26.8 MB, 4.1.12.0. Other programs listed: Microsoft 365 - en-us; Microsoft Edge; Microsoft Edge WebView2 Runtime; Microsoft OneDrive; Microsoft OneNote - en-us; Microsoft Visual C++ 2022 Redistributable (Arm64) - 14.38...; Microsoft Windows Desktop Runtime - 8.0.7 (x64); Remote Desktop Connection; X-Rite Color Assistant 2.49.0.]

FIGURE 13-4

TIP

After you install a program, take note of whether your computer runs differently. If your computer slows or behaves sluggishly, the program you recently installed could be the culprit. Uninstall it, if necessary.

8. You can uninstall programs only by using Control Panel. To uninstall an app, select the Search box on the taskbar and type the app's name. For example, type **muse** for the Audacity app you downloaded earlier.

9. In the search results, select Muse if necessary, and on the right side of the screen, select Uninstall if you want, as shown **in Figure 13-5**. As with programs, when you uninstall an app, it is removed from your computer. If you want the app back, you need to download and install it again.

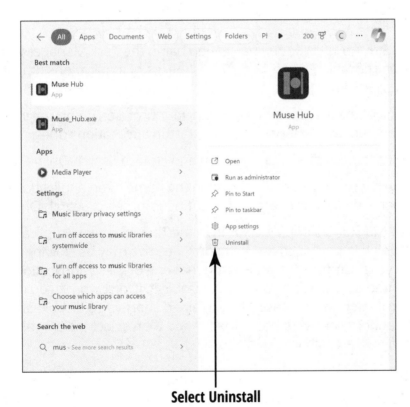

Select Uninstall

FIGURE 13-5

Control Startup Apps

1. Startup apps are applications that start running when you turn on your computer. You might be surprised by how many startup apps run in the background without your knowing it. Occasionally you install new software or download a program from the internet and discover that it runs automatically whether you like it or not. Sometimes the number of startup apps slows the computer down. To see which apps start running automatically when you turn on your computer, start the Task Manager with one of these techniques:

   - **Keyboard:** Press Ctrl+Alt+Del and select Task Manager on the blue screen.

   - **Search:** Select the search box on the taskbar, enter **task** in the Search box, and then select the Task Manager in the search results.

2. Select Startup apps on the navigation bar in the Task Manager window, as shown in **Figure 13-6**. This is the list of applications that start when your computer starts.

3. Use one of these techniques to open your browser, go on the internet, and find out what one of these startup applications does:

   - **Mouse:** Right-click an application and choose Search Online.

   - **Touchscreen:** Tap and hold down the name of an application. When a box appears around your fingertip, select Search Online.

4. Notice the Startup Impact column in the Task Manager. Applications with a high impact such as Microsoft OneDrive may be slowing down your computer. If you decide that one of these applications is unwanted or is slowing you down, disable it. (Don't worry; you can enable it later on very easily, as explained shortly.) To disable an application, select its name in the list and then select the Disable button on the toolbar.

TIP

To enable a startup application in the Task Manager (refer to **Figure 13-6**), select its name and then select the Enable button. The Status column in the Task Manager tells you whether a startup application has been disabled.

Startup apps

Disable

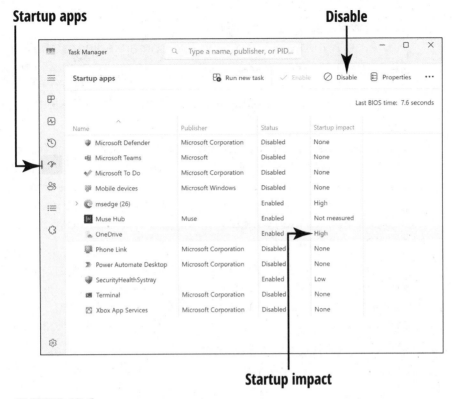

Startup impact

FIGURE 13-6

Explore System Information

1. Select the search box on the taskbar and type **control panel** in the Search box.

2. Select Control Panel in the Search results. In the Control Panel, select System and Security.

3. In the System and Security window, select System. The System window shown in **Figure 13-7** appears. This screen is chock-full of information and functions. (You need to scroll down the screen to see everything.) Note each of the following areas onscreen:

   - **Device Specifications:** This section displays details about your hardware, including the processor, the amount of installed memory (RAM), and other details.

- **Windows Specifications:** Of course, you have Windows 11. However, Windows 11 comes in two primary editions: the Home edition, which you are likely to have, and the Pro edition, for computer professionals. You may find information here about so-called Service or Experience Packs, which are large collections of updates to Windows 11.

- **Computer name, domain, and workgroup settings:** This information pertains to your network, if you have one. If a computer can't connect to a network, the problem is often related to the name of the Workgroup (a network). The Change Settings function lets you change the Workgroup name to match other computers on the same network.

TIP

Windows 11 gives your computer a nondescript, generic name to begin with. To give your computer a more descriptive name, select Rename this PC at the very top of the System window (refer to **Figure 13-7**). Enter a new name in the Rename Your PC dialog box.

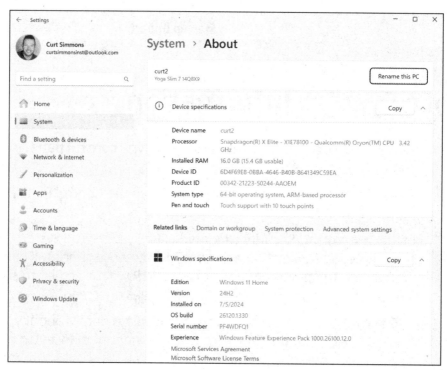

FIGURE 13-7

- **Product key and activation:** In an effort to control software piracy involving bootlegged copies of Windows 11, each copy of Windows 11 must be activated. Odds are that you activated your copy the first time you started your computer.

TIP

Don't be alarmed by the System information and options. If all goes well, you don't have to use most of what you find here. Some familiarity with this screen will be useful, however, if all doesn't go well later.

Check Your Security and Maintenance Status

1. In Control Panel, select System and Security, and on the next screen, choose Security and Maintenance (see **Figure 13-8**). The Security and Maintenance window appears, as shown in **Figure 13-9**.

TIP

Another way to open the Security and Maintenance window is to type **Security and Maintenance** using Search on the Windows taskbar.

FIGURE 13-8

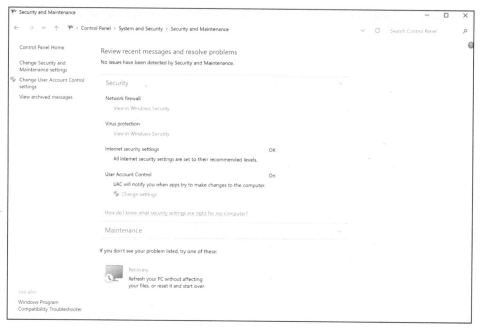

FIGURE 13-9

2. Note any message displayed under Review Recent Messages and Resolve Problems. Ideally, you see *No issues have been detected by Security and Maintenance.* If you see a message concerning a specific problem, select that message for more information.

3. Select the Security heading in the Security and Maintenance window. That section expands to detail security functions. Every option should display *On* or *OK*. Here's a brief description of each item under Security:

   - **Network Firewall:** The firewall scans internet traffic and blocks activity from programs that don't have explicit permission to use internet access. When you install a program that uses the internet, you may be asked to approve the connection the first time. The safest practice is to reject online connections that you don't initiate or recognize.

   - **Virus Protection:** Having virus protection for your computer is essential. Windows Defender, an antivirus protection program, comes with Windows 11, although you can install another antivirus program if you want. Later in this chapter, "Protect Your Computer from Viruses and Other Threats" explains how Windows Defender works.

- **Internet Security Settings:** These settings pertain to your browser. The default settings may be adequate.

- **User Account Control (UAC):** This function notifies you of programs that try to make changes to your system and requires that you confirm any such changes. In particular, UAC lets you know when a program tries to run or install software that may be malicious. When in doubt, say No or Cancel to UAC messages.

4. Select the Maintenance heading to see what that section includes. Functions under Maintenance consist of the following:

- **Report Problems:** This setting is on, allowing Windows 11 to regularly check for solutions to problems it uncovers. (In Step 5, you run the Reliability History report from this part of the screen.)

- **Automatic Maintenance:** Your computer automatically performs critical updates, security scans, and diagnostics each day.

TIP

If your computer is in a guest room or bedroom, you may want to change the Automatic Maintenance setting to run maintenance tasks at some time other than the default 3:00 a.m. Your computer may actually wake up at that hour for maintenance. (If your computer is connected to a power strip, however, you can turn off the power strip and prevent your computer from turning on automatically in the middle of the night.) If the computer can't run maintenance at the appointed hour, it will do so at the next opportunity.

- **Drive status:** *Drives* are hard disks inside or attached to your computer. Your documents, photos, and Windows 11 itself are stored on one or more drives. Ideally, the drive status is *All drives are working properly*. See Chapter 16 for information on backing up and restoring files.

- **Device software:** If a device on your computer needs a driver or other type of software to run properly, you are alerted here. (If no drivers are needed, you see the words *No action needed.*) Select Install Device Software to install the software.

TIP

The Security and Maintenance window is a troubleshooting tool, so you should check it if you have problems running Windows 11.

5. Under Report Problems, select View Reliability History. As shown in **Figure 13-10**, the Reliability Monitor screen graphs your computer's stability and indicates hardware and software problems, including those you may not be aware of. On this screen, red circles indicate critical events such as computer crashes; blue circles are information about software installation and updates; and yellow triangles indicate warnings about noncritical events (something that didn't crash the computer). Select a day in the graph to display details in the lower portion of the screen.

FIGURE 13-10

TIP

Reviewing the Reliability Monitor screen helps you distinguish between a one-time glitch and a recurring or worsening problem.

Speed Up Your Computer

1. Frequently used computers tend to slow down over time. However, Windows 11 offers a couple of administrative tools that can make your computer work faster. To find out what these tools are, select the Search box on the taskbar and type **windows tools** in the Search box. Then select the Windows Tools app in the search results. The Windows Tools app shows you a folder of tools you can use, as shown in **Figure 13-11**.

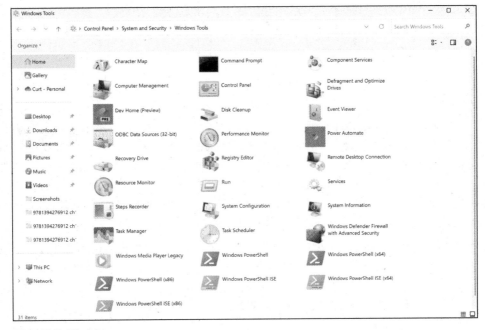

FIGURE 13-11

2. Select Defragment and Optimize Drives. The Optimize Drives screen opens, as shown in **Figure 13-12**. When you save a file, the new data you recently added gets placed on the hard drive wherever Windows 11 can find room for it. Consequently, a file is stored in many different places. If you've used your computer for a long time, files become fragmented — the bits and pieces are spread all over the drive, and your computer has to work hard to assemble all the pieces to open a file.

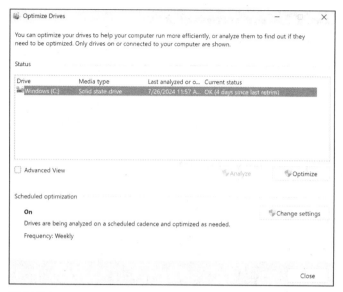

3. Select the C drive and then select the Optimize button. Windows 11 optimizes your hard drive by moving the bits and pieces of files so that they are stored next to each other on the hard drive. It can take a few minutes or a few hours to optimize a hard drive, but no matter, because Windows 11 conducts this activity in the background and you can go on to do other tasks.

4. Return to the Windows Tools screen (refer to **Figure 13-11**) and select Disk Cleanup. The Disk Cleanup for Windows dialog box appears, as shown in **Figure 13-13**. It tells you how much disk space you can make available on your hard drive by removing unnecessary files.

5. Select the types of files you want deleted, and then select the Clean Up System Files button. A message box appears as the files are deleted from your computer.

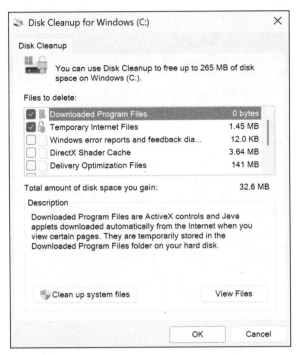

Disk Cleanup for Windows (C:)

Disk Cleanup

You can use Disk Cleanup to free up to 265 MB of disk space on Windows (C:).

Files to delete:

☑	Downloaded Program Files	0 bytes
☑	Temporary Internet Files	1.45 MB
☐	Windows error reports and feedback dia...	12.0 KB
☐	DirectX Shader Cache	3.64 MB
☐	Delivery Optimization Files	141 MB

Total amount of disk space you gain: 32.6 MB

Description

Downloaded Program Files are ActiveX controls and Java applets downloaded automatically from the Internet when you view certain pages. They are temporarily stored in the Downloaded Program Files folder on your hard disk.

Clean up system files   View Files

OK   Cancel

FIGURE 13-13

Protect Your Computer from Viruses and Other Threats

1. Windows can identify and remove viruses, spyware, and other malefactors from your computer. To refine how Windows secures your computer against outside threats, select the Search box on the taskbar and type **virus** in the Search box. In the Search results, choose Virus & Threat Protection. The Windows Security page opens, as shown in **Figure 13-14**. This page tells you whether the defense mechanisms on your computer are up to date. If they aren't up to date, you can take actions here to update your computer's defenses.

Scan options

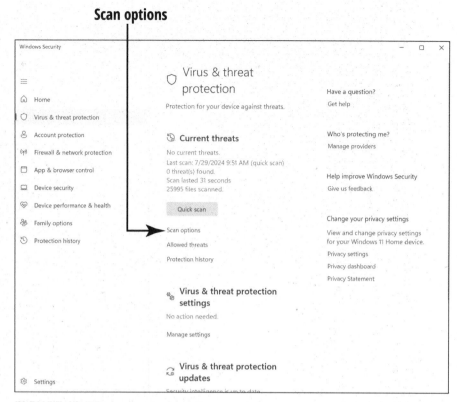

FIGURE 13-14

2. Windows performs "quick scans" in the background each time you run your computer. From time to time, to make sure your computer is thoroughly clean of viruses and spyware, run a full scan. Select the Scan Options link to display the scan options, shown in **Figure 13-15**. Then make sure that the Full Scan option is selected and select the Scan Now button.

3. A full scan can take a long time as Windows examines all the files on your computer for viruses and spyware. You can do other tasks on your computer while the full scan is running. If Windows finds a bad actor, the file with the virus or spyware is quarantined so that it won't harm your computer.

4. Close the Windows Security window.

FIGURE 13-15

IN THIS CHAPTER

» **Understanding plug-and-play hardware devices**

» **Setting up a printer**

» **Examining devices connected to your computer**

» **Fine-tuning a touchscreen**

Chapter **14**

Connecting a Printer and Other Devices

E very computer has a screen. Most computers, other than tablets, also have a keyboard and a mouse or other pointing device. You can add a mouse to a laptop that lacks one or replace the keyboard or mouse that came with your computer. Add a printer or a scanner to extend your computer's functionality.

For any hardware add-ons — which tech folk call *peripherals* — Windows 11 has a trick up its sleeve. Thanks to *plug-and-play* technology, which automatically identifies add-on devices, connecting new devices to your computer can be quite easy.

In this chapter, you explore the devices connected to your computer, as well as options available for those devices. You find out how to access devices connected to your computer and also calibrate a touchscreen to make it work better for you.

Trust USB Plug and Play for Hardware

You may find many kinds of add-on devices useful:

» A **printer** lets you, well, print documents and photos. Your choices for printers include black and white versus color, and inkjet versus laser printer. A multifunction printer also works as a copier, scanner, and fax machine.

» A **digital camera** captures photos that you can copy to your computer to enjoy and to share with others. See Chapter 11 for information on working with photos.

» A **scanner** enables you to make digital images of old photos or documents so that you can view them onscreen. Chapter 11 explains how to use a scanner.

» An **external hard drive** stores backup copies of your files. See Chapter 16 for information on adding an external hard drive to your computer.

» An additional or replacement **pointing device** (your mouse is a pointing device), including a trackball or a pen with a tablet, may be more comfortable to use than what came with your computer. Switching between pointing devices helps you avoid repetitive stress. A wireless mouse eliminates the hassle of dealing with a cord. Some people like to add a mouse as an alternative to their laptop's built-in touchpad.

» A **microphone** is crucial for communicating by voice with your computer through speech recognition, or with your friends over the internet. A combination headset with microphone may produce the clearest sound.

» A **video camera** (or *webcam*) is essential for video phone calls *à la* the Jetsons. See Chapter 11 for information on using a video camera.

Some of these devices are built into computers; some are not. Most devices that aren't built in connect to a computer using Universal Serial Bus (USB) technology. When you connect a device to your computer using a USB cable to the USB port (see **Figure 14-1**), the device identifies itself to the computer. This identification process is called *plug and play.* Ideally, you connect your device, and it simply works.

USB port   **USB cable**

FIGURE 14-1

Windows 11 uses a *device driver* to communicate with an add-on device. The driver is really a program that tells Windows 11 how to run the device. When you connect a device, such as a printer, Windows 11 looks for a driver (in this case, a *printer driver*). That driver may be built into Windows 11 or need to be downloaded from the internet, either automatically by Windows 11 or manually by you. Always take a look at the device's installation instructions to find out whether you need to download a driver from the manufacturer's website.

TIP

Every computer has at least one USB port. Some are in the front; others are in the side, back, or top of the computer and are harder to reach. If your computer doesn't have enough ports, you can add more by buying a USB hub, which is a small box with several USB ports. If a port is hard to reach with a device's cable, you can buy a USB extension cable. Office supply stores may have hubs and cables, or you can easily find them online.

TIP

If you have a newer computer, it may also have one or more USB-C ports. The USB-C is a newer type of USB connection that uses a smaller connector shape than the former USB and it's easier to plug in. Also, USB-C cables are much faster than USB. Consult your computer documentation for more details.

TIP

Just because you can plug something into your computer doesn't mean you should! Flash drives and other storage media that plug into your PC can also contain viruses, so be sure to use only items from trusted sources. In other words, if you find a flash drive on the sidewalk, don't take it home and plug it into your computer!

TIP

Bluetooth is a wireless technology for adding devices to your computer. If your computer has Bluetooth, you can use Bluetooth as well as USB to add some devices, such as a microphone, headset, or wireless keyboard and mouse.

See All Devices

1. Select the Search box on the taskbar and type **settings** in the Search box; then click the Settings app that appears in the search results. The Settings window opens. Choose Bluetooth & Devices to open the Bluetooth & Devices window, as shown in **Figure 14-2**. Devices listed may include your monitor, speakers, headphones, keyboard, mouse, and more. Devices shared through your network (if your computer is connected to a network) also appear here. For information on adjusting device settings, see the "Access Device Options" section, later in the chapter.

2. Select the Printers & Scanners category in the Bluetooth & Devices window to see the screen shown in **Figure 14-3**. This screen lists printers and scanners that are connected to your computer.

TIP

Some, but not all, devices display information below the device name. A network device may display *Offline* (which means not accessible) or it may display nothing if it is accessible. A printer may display *Ready* or it may display nothing if the printer isn't ready.

FIGURE 14-2

FIGURE 14-3

TIP

You are unlikely to need the Add a Bluetooth or Other Device button because most devices are added *automagically* (that's a word nerds like to use). However, if you select Add a Device, Windows 11 scans for additional hardware that you may have connected to the computer. No harm in doing so.

Connect a Printer or Other Device

1. Take your printer out of the box. Keep all the packing material together until you know you won't need to return the printer. Arrange all the components for easy access. In addition to the printer, you'll probably find ink cartridges or a toner cartridge, a power cable, and some basic installation instructions. Read the setup instructions that come with your printer before you do anything else!

TIP

Some of these steps apply to other devices, such as a mouse, a webcam, or a microphone. Printers often have more packaging and require more assembly than other devices.

TIP

Most printers connect wirelessly to your home internet router. That way, you can wirelessly print from any computer, tablet, or even your phone. If you need to connect the printer to your computer using a USB cable, you'll need to buy one because USB cables aren't typically included with the printer. Fortunately, they are cheap and available at most big-box stores or online.

2. Remove all tape from the printer. Most printers ship with the print mechanism locked in place to prevent it from moving during shipping. Look for brightly colored tape, paper, or plastic indicating what you need to move or remove to release the print mechanism.

3. Put the printer within cable length of your computer if you're not using a wireless printer. Insert the ink or toner cartridge before you turn on the printer for the first time. Place some paper in the paper drawer or tray. Connect the printer to the power supply. Plug the printer cable into the printer and into the computer. If you're using a wireless printer, follow the setup instructions for connecting the computer to your internet router.

TIP

Very likely, you have to download and install a software program from your printer's manufacturer in order to install your printer. Chapter 13 describes how to install programs from a company website.

4. Turn on the printer. A notification tells you that Windows is "setting up a device." If all goes well, you soon see this notification: *Device is ready,* your printer (the brand and model number of your printer) *is set up and ready to go.* You may see other informational messages as Windows 11 handles the configuration, and you may see messages from the printer software as well. Just follow the printer manufacturer's instructions as needed.

5. To confirm that your printer is installed properly, see the preceding section, "See All Devices."

Access Device Options

1. You can often make adjustments to some devices, which affect how they work and behave. To access these options, type **settings** in the Search box on the taskbar and choose Settings in the results; then choose Bluetooth & Devices. If you scroll down, you see different categories, such as Devices, Printers & Scanners, Cameras, and so forth, as shown in **Figure 14-4**.

2. Select the Printers & Scanners category, which opens a window showing printers or scanners installed on your computer.

TIP

Windows 11 automatically installs the Microsoft Print to PDF software. This software doesn't print but does create files that you can print later using a real printer. For example, if you're in a coffee shop and want to print a web page or an email message, you can use this device and then open the file it creates when your computer is connected to a printer.

3. Select the device you want to examine. This action opens the device's properties in a window with options. **Figure 14-5** shows information about a printer. Here, you can open the print queue, print a test page, or access additional printer properties. When you're finished reviewing the information or selecting available options, return to the previous screen by clicking the back arrow on the toolbar.

FIGURE 14-4

FIGURE 14-5

TIP

If a test page doesn't print, check that both ends of the cable are plugged in properly and make sure the printer is turned on. If you're using a wireless printer, make sure the printer is connected to your internet router. Try to print a test page again. For more help, contact the printer manufacturer or the store where you bought the printer, or search the web.

TIP

The top of the Bluetooth & Devices window has the Add Device button, but you need to use it only if Windows 11 doesn't automatically detect and install your device. With USB and plug-and-play technology, most devices install automatically.

Adjust Your Touchscreen

1. You can make some adjustments to your computer's touchscreen (if you have one). By default, the touchscreen mimics what a mouse does in terms of single-clicking and double-clicking; instead, you single-tap or double-tap on the screen. You can adjust the double-tap settings in particular. Select the Search box on the taskbar and type **control panel** in the Search box. Select Control Panel in the search results and then select Hardware and Sound in the Control Panel window. You see the Hardware and Sound window, shown in **Figure 14-6**.

2. In the Hardware and Sound window, select Change Touch Input Settings (it's under Pen and Touch); see **Figure 14-6**. The Pen and Touch dialog box appears.

3. On the Touch tab, select Settings. This action opens the Double-Tab settings window (**Figure 14-7**).

4. You have two options here. You can use the two slider bars to adjust how quickly you tab the screen when you double-tap, or you can adjust the distance the pointer can move between tapping when you double-tap. By default, these settings are in the middle of Slow and Fast on each slider bar. To adjust them, just move the slider bars as desired.

5. When you're done, notice the Test Settings at the bottom of the window. You can double-tap the image to see how the screen responds to your double-tap. You can then go back and make adjustments to the Speed and Spatial Tolerance slider bars if necessary. When you're done, click OK.

FIGURE 14-6

FIGURE 14-7

Chapter **15**

Working with Files

All the data inside your computer is stored on a disk. Your computer has a primary disk, formally called the internal *hard drive.* You may see this disk referred to as the C drive. (The terms *drive* and *disk* are interchangeable.)

The contents of a disk are organized into individual files. When you create a file and save it for the first time, you create a file on a disk. Many other files on the disk belong to the programs you use, including the thousands of files that make up Windows 11.

Disks also are organized into *folders,* which are containers for files. For its own files, Windows 11 has a main folder that contains dozens of other folders (called *subfolders*). Inside or below that user account folder, Windows 11 creates more folders to help you organize your files by type. For example, by default, all your photos go into the Pictures folder, and all your documents go into the Documents folder.

In this chapter, you discover how to save and open a file, search for files, and explore your disk, folders, and files. You work with File Explorer as you create new folders to organize documents and move files from one folder to another. You also copy files from your hard drive to other disks to take with you or give to other people. This chapter also explains how to rename and delete files and folders. What if you delete a file or folder and you regret doing so? Don't worry, because this chapter shows you how to get back a file or folder that you mistakenly deleted.

Save and Open a File

1. In computer land, nothing is more important than files. Computer programs are stored in files. Data is stored in files. To start working, you open a file. When you're finished working, you save and close your file. To experiment with files, open Notepad, a text-editing app that comes with Windows 11.

TIP

Chapter 2 explains how to open apps. Chapter 9 looks into the details of Notepad.

2. As shown in **Figure 15-1**, type a few words into Notepad and then save your file. Most apps (Notepad included) offer a couple of ways to save a file:

   - Press Ctrl+S.

   - Open the File menu and choose Save.

3. When you save a file for the first time, the Save As dialog box appears (refer to **Figure 15-1**). It invites you to give the file a name and to tell Windows 11 which folder to keep it in. Enter the name **My File** in the File Name text box. The Save As dialog box offers the means of choosing a folder for your file. For now, you can store your file in the Documents folder, the folder that Windows 11 selected for you (refer to **Figure 15-1**). Notice that the Documents folder is already selected in the navigation pane on the left side of the Save As dialog box.

4. Select the Save button in the Save As dialog box. Congratulations! You just saved your file. The title tab at the top of the Notepad window shows the name of your file, "My File." When you're not sure what a file is called, look at the title tab or bar along the top of the screen.

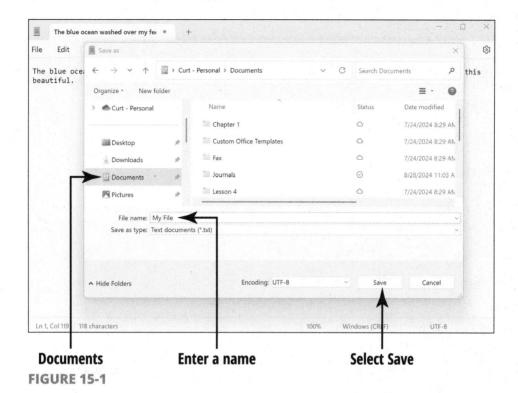

Documents   **Enter a name**   **Select Save**

FIGURE 15-1

5. Close Notepad. The fastest way to close an app is to select the Close button (the *X*) in the upper-right corner of the screen.

6. Open Notepad as you did in Step 1. Where is My File, the file you saved and named in Steps 4 and 5?

7. Open the File menu (select the word *File* in the upper-left corner of the screen) and choose Open. The Open dialog box appears, as shown in **Figure 15-2**. This dialog box is the mirror image of the Save As dialog box that you saw earlier. Use it to locate the file you want to open. In this case, Windows 11 has opened the dialog box to its favorite folder, Documents, which also happens to be the folder where My File is stored.

8. Choose My File and then select the Open button (refer to **Figure 15-2**). My File opens onscreen.

TIP

Most apps offer shortcuts for opening files. For example, you may see a list of files that you recently opened on the File menu. You can select a filename on the list to open a file straightaway.

Select a folder

Select a file   **Select Open**

FIGURE 15-2

Find a Misplaced File

1. To search for a misplaced file, begin with the Search box, located on the taskbar. Type the name of a document or photo you have on your computer. The search results appear, as shown in **Figure 15-3**.

TIP

Initially, the search results show all and sundry — settings, apps, files, websites, and other search opportunities. If you don't see the item you want in a search, narrow the list of items by selecting one of the tabs at the top of the search window — Apps, Documents, Web, or More. Documents, for example, narrows the search to items on your computer.

2. To open a file, select it in the search results. If more than one application on your computer is capable of opening the file, you may see the Select an App to Open This File? dialog box, as shown in **Figure 15-4**. Select an application to open the file.

Narrow the search

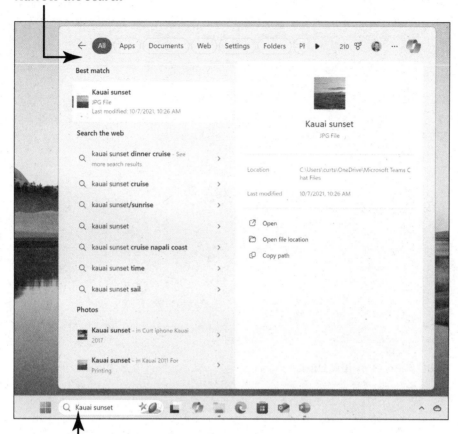

Enter a search term

FIGURE 15-3

TIP

The Select an App to Open This File dialog box offers a means of telling Windows 11 to always open files of a certain type with a particular application (refer to **Figure 15-4**). Selecting the Always button tells Windows 11 to open files of a certain type automatically with the app you chose. You can also select the Just Once button to have this particular app open the file this time. The Just Once option is a good one if you don't want the app to become the default app for opening this kind of file.

3. Close the app that opens the file by using one of these methods:

- Click or tap the Close button (the X located in the upper-right corner of the screen).

- Press Alt+F4.

Choose an application

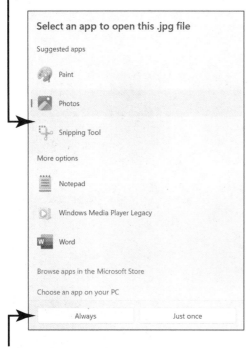

Select an app to open this .jpg file

Suggested apps

Paint

Photos

Snipping Tool

More options

Notepad

Windows Media Player Legacy

Word

Browse apps in the Microsoft Store

Choose an app on your PC

| Always | Just once |

Select Always or Just Once

FIGURE 15-4

TIP

Strictly speaking, if you find what you're looking for, stop look-ing. (No extra charge for pearls of wisdom.) In this case, however, keep looking, because doing so reveals important information about how files are organized and how you can take control of that organization.

4. On the taskbar, select the File Explorer icon (the yellow folder). File Explorer opens. Notice that File Explorer contains a toolbar, a left navigation pane, and a right content pane that displays the contents of the selected folder, as shown in **Figure 15-5**.

5. Select the Home folder on the left side of the File Explorer window, and then select the box labeled *Search* (probably followed by *Home*) to the right of the toolbar. Type the same search term that you used in Step 1. As you type, File Explorer displays any matching files, high-lighting the text that matches. **Figure 15-6** shows the results of a search on a computer using the search term *Kauai sunset*.

Toolbar

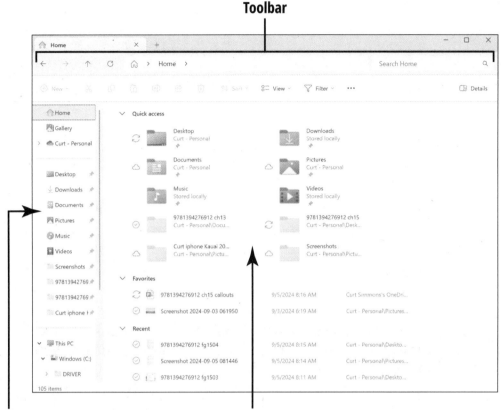

Navigation pane　　　　　　　　**Contents pane**

FIGURE 15-5

TIP

On a touchscreen, the virtual keyboard doesn't appear on the desktop until you select the keyboard icon on the right side of the taskbar.

TIP

If the search results include too many files, thereby making it hard to see the one you want, type more of the filename in the Search box. The number of matching files should decrease as you type more text in the box.

6. The *focus* of a search — where File Explorer searches — determines what files and folders are found. In Step 5, you selected This PC, making all the files on your computer the focus of the search. Accordingly, Windows 11 searched for files and folders throughout your computer. To change the focus of your search to the Pictures folder, select the Pictures folder in the navigation pane. Then select the box labeled Search and enter your search term again. The search results focus on files in the Pictures folder.

FIGURE 15-6

TIP

You can use the Sort feature on the toolbar to refine a search as needed. Start a search and then click Sort ⇨ More. You can then choose to sort by date created, authors, tags, and so forth.

Add a Location to Quick Access

1. If you frequently access a specific location using File Explorer, you might want to add that location to the Quick Access section of the Home folder. Select Home in the navigation pane. In the content pane, the first section of the Home folder is Quick Access. Windows 11 places some folders in the Quick Access folder list automatically, including the Documents folder and the Pictures folder. As well, it lists in alphabetical order folders that you visit frequently.

TIP

You may need to expand the Quick Access option to see the folders. To do so, click or tap the arrow next to Quick Access in the navigation pane to expand it, as shown in **Figure 15-7**.

Select Home   **Click to expand Quick Access**

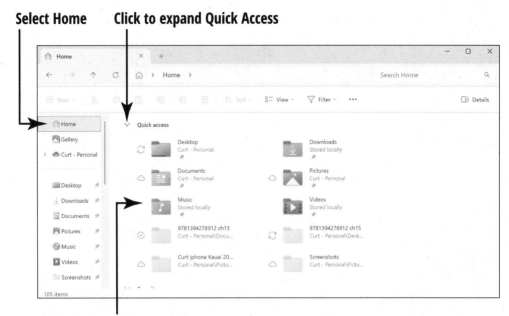

Quick Access folder and files

FIGURE 15-7

2. Select a folder that you access frequently. For example, if you're currently working on files that you keep in a folder called My Work, select that folder in the navigation pane.

3. On the See More button on the toolbar (it looks like three dots), select the Pin to Quick Access option on the menu (refer to **Figure 15-8**). The name of the folder you selected in Step 2 now appears in the Quick Access folder list. Notice the pin beside or under its name.

4. Select your folder in the Quick Access folder list. Next time you want to get to this folder, you can get there quickly by selecting Home in the navigation pane and then selecting your folder from the Quick Access list.

TIP

To remove a folder from the Quick Access list, select the folder you want to remove. Then right-click the folder and choose Unpin from Quick Access on the shortcut menu.

Select the desired file or folder   **Select See More**

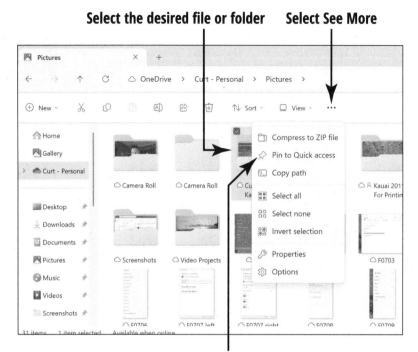

Select Pin to Quick Access

FIGURE 15-8

Use File Explorer for Easy Access to Files

1. Select the File Explorer icon on the taskbar if File Explorer is not already open.

TIP

The keyboard shortcut to open File Explorer is ⌘+E.

2. On the left, select Documents, then Music, and then Pictures, and then Videos, while noting the files in the content pane on the right. Many Windows 11 apps store files by default in the Documents, Music, Pictures, and Videos folders. Select the Documents folder again.

3. To create a practice document that you can use in later sections, select the New button on the toolbar. On the menu that appears, select Text Document, as shown in **Figure 15-9**. (If you don't see this option, make sure that the Documents folder is selected.) An empty text document is created and the words *New Text Document* are highlighted so that you can type a new name. Type **practice file**. (You'll rename this file in a later section.) Feel free to repeat this step to create additional items for practice. You can create different kinds of files based on the app and programs installed on your PC.

TIP

On a touchscreen, the virtual keyboard doesn't appear on the desktop until you select the keyboard icon on the right side of the taskbar.

4. Select the View button on the taskbar. In the drop-down menu that appears, select each option, such as Extra Large Icons and Large, Medium, and Small Icons. Try them all if you like.

Select New

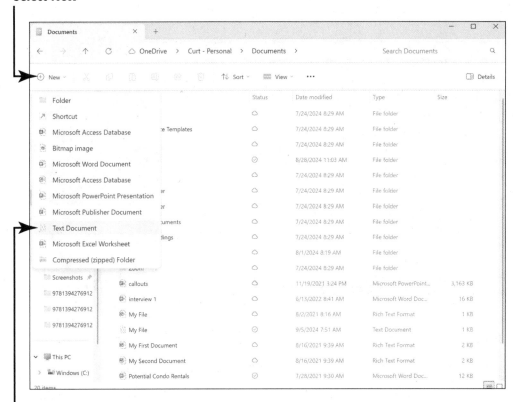

Select Text Document

FIGURE 15-9

Certain layouts are better for certain purposes. For example, photos are easier to recognize as Extra Large Icons than as a List. **Figure 15-10** shows documents using the Details view, which includes the date the file was modified.

TIP

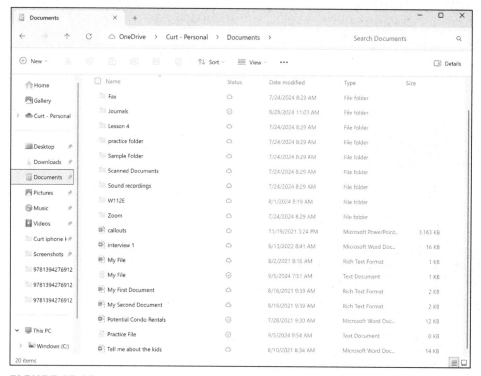

FIGURE 15-10

Create a Folder to Organize Your Files

1. In the File Explorer navigation pane, select the Documents folder.

2. Select the New button on the taskbar and choose Folder from the drop-down menu. An icon for the new folder appears in the contents area on the right, with the name *New folder* next to it and already selected (see **Figure 15-11**).

On a touchscreen, the virtual keyboard doesn't appear on the desktop until you select the keyboard icon on the right side of the taskbar.

TIP

Select New and choose Folder   **A new folder appears**

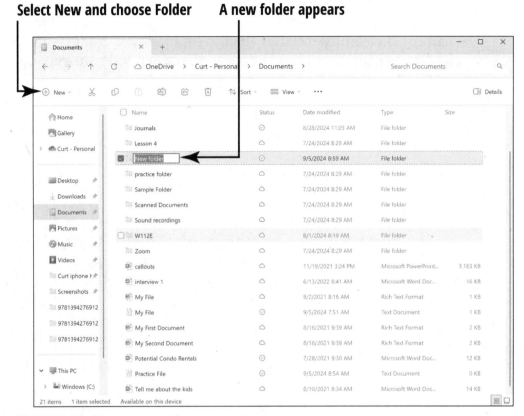

FIGURE 15-11

3. Type **practice folder** as the new name. Don't move the cursor or mouse before you start typing. Your new text will replace the high-lighted text automatically. Press the Enter key to make the new name stick. (If you have a problem naming the folder, see the "Rename a File or a Folder" section, later in this chapter.)

4. Open your new folder by double-clicking or double-tapping its icon. Notice that the content pane is empty.

5. To return to the Documents folder, select Documents in the naviga-tion pane.

TIP

Don't worry too much about creating folders, because the folders that Windows 11 provides may be all you ever need. As you accu-mulate more files, however, placing them into other folders can help you stay organized. In the Documents folder, for example, you might create a subfolder called Finances for files related to income, expenses, and investments, and another subfolder called Family for family-related documents. Which folders and sub-folders to create and how to name them depends entirely on your own sense of order.

Use Check Boxes to Select Files

1. In File Explorer, you select files to move, copy, rename, or delete. You can add a check box to make selecting multiple files easier. This option may be turned on by default. Select a file or folder in File Explorer, and if a check box appears next to it, you don't need to do anything else. If not, however, you can turn on this feature. In File Explorer, select the View button on the toolbar and then select Show. Click the Item Check Boxes option on the menu that appears, as shown in **Figure 15-12**.

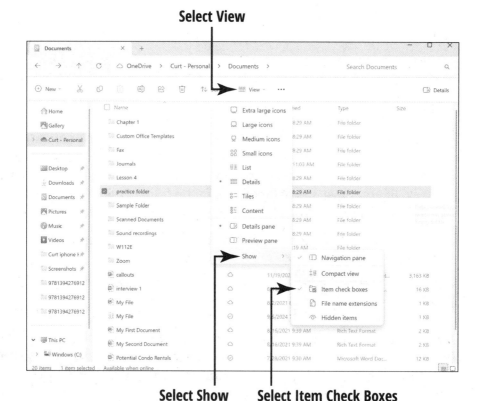

Select View

Select Show   **Select Item Check Boxes**

FIGURE 15-12

2. Select the Documents folder (or any folder that contains more than one file). To select a file, click or tap its filename. (You won't see the check box until you select it with a tap or a click, or hover over it with the mouse pointer.) Repeat to select additional files. If you want to deselect a file, select the check box again to remove the check mark. Close the window after you've seen how these check boxes work. **Figure 15-13** shows four selected files.

TIP

If you want to select only a single file, you can select anywhere on the filename. You use the check box when you want to select more than one file at a time.

The See More button on the toolbar offers other methods for selecting. Select All does just what it says — selects all objects in a folder or library. Select None works similarly. Invert Selection switches the selection. For example, if you chose Invert Selection in the context of **Figure 15-13**, the four selected files would be deselected and all the other files would be selected. Sometimes it's easier to select the files you don't want and then invert the selection.

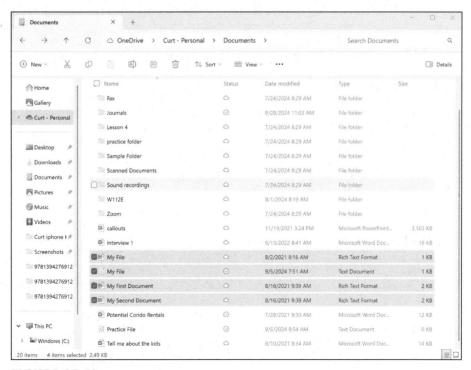

FIGURE 15-13

Undo or Redo an Action

1. Sometimes you make mistakes when you're working with Windows 11. For example, you may give a file the wrong name or move a file to the wrong folder. The good news is that you can easily undo your last action. Just click the See More button on the toolbar and you see Undo in the menu list, as shown in **Figure 15-14**.

2. If you make a mistake and want to undo your last action, just click the Undo button. Note that there is no time limit for Undo, so no rush. However, also note that Undo undoes only your last action. You can't use this feature to undo something you did several steps back as you're working in File Explorer.

   TIP The keyboard shortcut for undo is Ctrl+Z.

3. You can also redo an action that you've chosen to undo. Say you undo a filename for a document, but then you realize that the original file name was correct after all. In that case, just select See More and then select Redo, as shown in **Figure 15-14**.

FIGURE 15-14

TIP

The keyboard shortcut for redo is Ctrl+Y.

Move a File from One Folder to Another

1. You can move files to organize them. For this exercise, select the Documents folder in File Explorer. Select one of your documents.

TIP

To move more than one file at a time, see the section "Use Check Boxes to Select Files," earlier in this chapter.

2. In the navigation pane, scroll to find the folder you want to move the file to. When you see it, just drag the file to the new folder in the navigation pane and release it. This action moves the file out of the original folder and to the new folder you've chosen.

TIP

Use these same steps to move a subfolder from one folder to another. However, don't move folders that Windows 11 creates.

Rename a File or a Folder

1. You can change the name of any file or folder you create. (Don't rename files in the Windows or Program Files folders.) For this exercise, select the Documents folder in File Explorer. Then select one of your files.

TIP

To rename more than one file at a time, see the section "Use Check Boxes to Select Files," earlier in this chapter. On completion of the rename operation, the files you selected will share the name you provide; each file will have a unique number added to the name, starting with *(1)*.

2. On the toolbar, select the Rename button. In the content pane, the current name of the file or folder is selected, as shown in **Figure 15-15**. If you type anything while the text is selected, you erase the current name, which is convenient if the new name is completely different from the old name. If you want to keep most of the current name and edit it, select inside the name or press the left- or right-arrow key to move to the place in the name where you want to type new text.

3. Type the new name, which can be more than 200 characters long (although a dozen characters may be more than enough). You can capitalize letters and use spaces and dashes, but you can't use slashes or asterisks, which Windows 11 reserves for other purposes.

TIP

On a touchscreen, the virtual keyboard doesn't appear on the desktop until you select the keyboard icon on the right side of the taskbar.

4. When you've typed the new name, press the Enter key to finish the process.

Type a new name   **Select Rename**

FIGURE 15-15

TIP

You can right-click a file's icon to see the Rename option on the context menu that appears. You may find this method faster.

Delete a File or Folder

TIP

1. You can delete any of your files that you no longer need. (Don't delete files in the Windows or Program Files folders.) For this exercise, select the Documents folder in File Explorer. Then select one of your files.

   To delete more than one file at a time, see the section "Use Check Boxes to Select Files," earlier in this chapter.

TIP

2. On the toolbar, select the Delete button.

   The keyboard shortcut to delete the selected file is the Delete key (surprise!).

3. A confirmation dialog box appears and asks whether you really want to delete the file, as shown in **Figure 15-16**. Here's your chance to change your mind if you want. However, for this exercise, select Yes in the dialog box to delete the file.

TIP

   If you don't see a confirmation dialog box like the one in **Figure 15-16**, tell Windows 11 that you want to see this dialog box when you delete files and folders. Just right-click the Recycle Bin and click Properties. On the Properties dialog box, select Display Delete Confirmation Dialog and click OK, as shown in **Figure 15-17**.

4. Select another file, and then select the Delete button. The Delete File confirmation window appears. This time, select No to cancel the operation.

FIGURE 15-16

Select this check box and click OK

FIGURE 15-17

Get Back a File or Folder You Deleted

1. Normally, when you delete a file or folder, Windows 11 moves the object to the Recycle Bin. Objects remain in the Recycle Bin indefinitely, allowing you to restore something you deleted long after you did so. To open the Recycle Bin, go to the desktop and double-click or double-tap the Recycle Bin icon. The Recycle Bin opens, as shown in **Figure 15-18**.

2. If many files or folders are listed in the Recycle Bin window, type the name of the item you want in the Search box in the top-right corner of the window. If any files match what you type, they appear in the content pane.

   Note that on a touchscreen, the virtual keyboard doesn't appear on the desktop until you select the keyboard icon on the right side of the taskbar.

Select the file you
want to restore

Select Restore the
Selected Items

Select See More

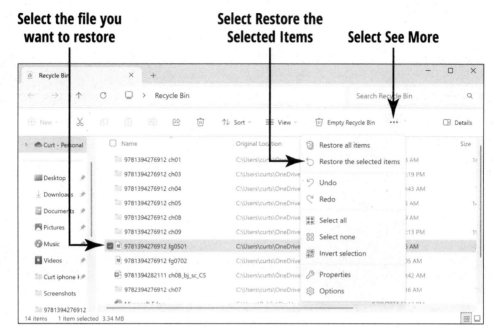

FIGURE 15-18

3. To restore a file or folder to its original location, select the file or folder in the Recycle Bin window. Select See More on the toolbar and select Restore the Selected Items. The selected file or folder returns to the folder it was in before it was deleted.

TIP

If Windows 11 needs disk space, it will automatically clear out the oldest files in the Recycle Bin first. If you want to get rid of everything in the Recycle Bin, select Empty Recycle Bin on the toolbar. After you empty the Recycle Bin, you can't undo your action.

TIP

Don't select the Restore All Items button, because doing so puts every single item in the Recycle Bin back in its original location. Most of the files in the Recycle Bin are probably files that you really meant to delete. Choosing this command would be like dumping the trash can on your living-room floor to find a penny you threw away.

See Chapter 16 for information on backing up and restoring files.

IN THIS CHAPTER

» **Backing up your computer**

» **Copying files to a removable drive**

» **Managing files on OneDrive**

» **Restoring a failed computer**

Chapter **16**

Backing Up and Restoring Files

S ome of your files — photos and documents — are priceless. If you accidentally delete a treasured file, what can you do but cry? You can ensure your well-being by creating copies of your documents and photos.

The best insurance involves storing copies of files on devices separate from your computer. Such devices include the following:

» **Flash drive and memory card:** Carry your files when you're away from your computer by storing them on a portable storage device. For example, you can store files on a USB *flash drive* (also called a *thumb drive*), or a *memory card,* which is the size of a postage stamp and is most often used in laptop computers and digital cameras. Common capacities for flash drives and memory cards range from 8GB to 1TB.

TIP

A *gigabyte* (GB) of storage can hold thousands of files, but you'll be amazed by how quickly you can fill that space. A *terabyte* (TB) is 1,000 gigabytes!

» **External hard drive:** This type of drive has a much higher capacity than a flash drive, making it ideal for backing up all your files — the best insurance. Affordable external hard drives range from 500GB to 3TB.

Two to 3TB of storage should be enough room to back up everything on your computer.

» **Network drive:** If your computer connects to a home network, you may be able to copy files to other devices on the network. For example, you can use a large-capacity network drive to back up files from more than one computer.

» **OneDrive:** Your Microsoft account comes with 5 gigabytes of free storage in the cloud (which means on the internet). Anything stored in OneDrive is duplicated on additional computers you log in to with the same Microsoft account.

OneDrive provides storage but not a backup (duplicate). If you delete a file from OneDrive, any copies stored on linked computers are also deleted.

In this chapter, you back up your entire computer as well as copy specific files to a flash drive or hard drive so that you can transport files between machines. You also find out how to store files in the Microsoft cloud with OneDrive. Consider this scenario: You write a letter to a friend and save it to your Documents folder. Later that day, you delete part of the letter and save it again, replacing the original document. The next day, you wish you still had the deleted text. The Backup function comes to your rescue because it saves versions of files; you can recover the latest version or an earlier version of a file. As I wrote this book, I saved it hundreds of times — the Backup function could save every version, allowing me to roll back to an earlier copy, to before I made some big goof. (That's purely hypothetical, of course.)

Finally, in this chapter, you explore the Reset function, a tool you may need if you have problems with your computer. The Reset function reinstalls Windows 11 but preserves your personal data.

Back Up Your Computer

1. To back up your computer, type **Windows Backup** in the Search box on the taskbar. Select Windows Backup in the search results. Before you back up your files, you need to

- **Sign in to your Microsoft account.** The backup tool uses OneDrive, so you have to be signed in to your Microsoft account to access the storage space Microsoft gives you. You're probably already signed in, but if not, see Chapter 10 to find out how to sign in.

- **Sign in to OneDrive.** As with your Microsoft account, you're probably already signed in, but if not, click the OneDrive icon in the notification area (which is on the taskbar near the date and time and looks like a cloud). Sign in with your Microsoft account.

TIP

Windows Backup is a simple way to use OneDrive, but know that Windows Backup and OneDrive have the same purpose: to keep your files safe. You can find out more about OneDrive in the "Use OneDrive to Store File Copies" section, later in this chapter.

2. In the Windows Backup window, you see four selection categories that you can click to expand. Under each, you can choose what you want to back up, as shown in **Figure 16-1**. Here are your options:

- **Folders:** You can back up files from your desktop as well as your Documents and Pictures folders here.

- **Apps:** Backup any apps on your PC using this option.

- **Settings:** This option copies all your Windows settings and preferences.

- **Credentials:** This option backs up your accounts, Wi-Fi networks, and other passwords.

TIP

I recommend that you backup everything! Choose every option here and let Windows keep a backup for you.

3. When you're ready, click the **Back Up** button on the Windows Backup window. Windows starts the backup process, and that's all you need to do. If you add new files or make changes, don't worry. Windows automatically keeps track of those changes and backs them up without any help.

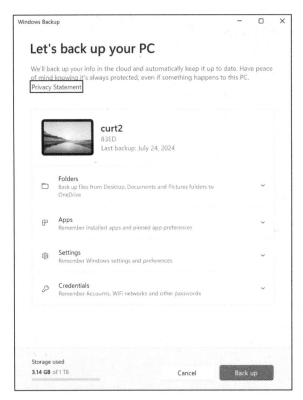

FIGURE 16-1

4. Windows 11 displays a *Choose what to do with removable drives* notification. (You can click the mouse instead of tapping.) If you select the first option, a list of choices appears, such as *Open folder to view files.* If you know which action you want to take, you can select that action. Otherwise, select Take No Action or wait until the notification disappears on its own.

Add an External Hard Drive or Flash Drive

1. Before you attach a flash drive or hard drive to your computer, consider the following options that Windows 11 automatically offers for using the newly attached removable drive:

- **Configure Storage Settings** opens the Settings app so that you can configure the storage settings on your computer.

- **Open Folder to View Files** displays the contents of the disk in File Explorer on the desktop. You select this option to copy files to or from the drive you're attaching.

- **Take No Action** dismisses the notification.

TIP

Notifications appear for the amount of time specified in PC Settings. If the notification disappears before you can select it, you can redisplay it by removing and then reinserting the drive or USB cable.

2. Locate an unused USB port on your computer. A *USB port* is a small rectangular slot on the front or back of a desktop computer or along any edge of a laptop or tablet computer. Your computer may support standard USB devices or USB-C devices (or both). USB-C is a newer USB port that is shaped differently from the older USB. If your computer supports only USB-C, you need to buy USB-C flash or hard drives, or you need an adapter to plug in an older USB device.

TIP

If a USB port is hard to reach, you can buy an extension cable from any office supply store. You can also buy a *hub,* which adds ports to your computer.

3. If you're using a flash drive, insert it into the USB slot. USB fits one way only. If you're using an external hard drive, plug it into a power source, if one is required, and then connect a cable to the USB port. Turn on the external drive, if it has a separate power switch. (Flash drives and some external hard drives don't have separate power supplies or switches.)

4. Windows 11 displays a *Choose what to do with removable drives* notification. (You can click the mouse instead of tapping.) If you select the first option, a list of choices appears, such as *Open folder to view files*. If you know which action you want to take, you can select that action. Otherwise, select Take No Action or wait until the notification disappears on its own.

Copy Files to or from a Flash Drive

1. To copy files or folders to a flash drive, insert the flash drive into one of your computer's USB ports.

   Laptops, like cameras, often have a slot for a memory card. Want to turn your memory card into a flash drive? Simply buy a device called a dedicated or single-purpose memory card reader. Strictly speaking, a multipurpose card reader also works, but multicard readers cost more and are often larger than single-card readers. In addition, a dedicated memory card reader doesn't need a cable to connect a camera to a computer. You can just download your pictures from the card to your hard drive.

2. If Windows 11 displays a notification when you insert the flash drive or memory card, select Open Folder to View Files, which will open File Explorer on the desktop. If File Explorer doesn't open automatically, go to the desktop and then select the yellow folder icon in the taskbar to open File Explorer.

   The keyboard shortcut to open File Explorer is ⌘+E.

3. In File Explorer, navigate on the left to the folder that contains the files you want to copy. See Chapter 15 for information on navigating in File Explorer. Select the folder.

4. On the right side of File Explorer, select the folder or file you want to copy. If you see a check box to the left of each object you want to copy, you can select each check box to copy multiple files simultaneously. (If you don't see check boxes next to files, see Chapter 15 for information on enabling this function for file selection.)

   To select every object on the right simultaneously, use the Select All button available on the See More menu.

   The keyboard shortcut to select all files in File Explorer is Ctrl+A.

5. Select the Copy button, as shown in **Figure 16-2**.

Copy

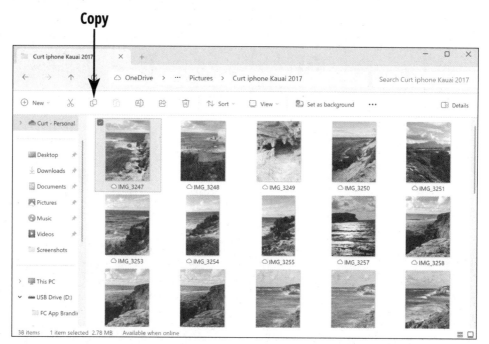

FIGURE 16-2

6. Click the little arrow next to This PC in the File Explorer navigation pane and locate the flash drive or memory card. The drive will not be Local Disk (C:), where Windows 11 resides. Select the removable flash drive or memory card to which you want to copy the files, and then select the folder you want to copy to, as shown in **Figure 16-3**. Then select the Paste button on the toolbar. If the files copy quickly, you may not see any indication of progress; otherwise, a progress bar is displayed until copying is complete.

TIP

OneDrive may be listed in the Copy Items window. Files you copy to OneDrive are automatically copied to the cloud and to linked computers.

7. If you copy a file that is already on the destination disk, the Replace or Skip Files window appears, as shown in **Figure 16-4**. (Perhaps you're copying a newer version of a file you copied before.) Note the available options:

- **Replace the File in the Destination:** Selecting this option replaces one file with another. Be certain that you don't need the replaced file (as you might if you want to keep different versions of files).

USB Drive **Paste**

FIGURE 16-3

FIGURE 16-4

- **Skip This File:** Selecting this option does nothing with this file.
- **Compare Info for Both Files:** Selecting this option opens another window in which you can select files on the left to replace those on the right, and select files on the right to keep. Selecting the same file on the left and right creates a second file with a number added

to the name, such as *my file (2)*. This option enables you to have the original and the new file.

Select one of the previous options. If you selected Compare Info for Both Files, select the files to replace or skip, and then select the Continue button. You may or may not see a progress indicator, depending on how quickly the files are copied.

8. Confirm that the copy worked by navigating on the left to the location you selected as the destination in Step 6. If the files are there, congratulations; you're done. If not, try Steps 4 through 6 again.

9. Remove the flash drive or memory card you inserted in Step 1. You're good to go.

If you have files or folders that you'd be devastated to lose, follow the steps in this task to create backup copies of those items on a portable storage device. Then keep that device in a safe place.

TIP

To copy files from a flash drive or memory card, follow these same steps, but select the flash drive in Step 3 and the folder or other destination to which you want to copy or move files in Step 6.

TIP

Use OneDrive to Store File Copies

1. Use OneDrive to back up and store files on the Microsoft cloud — in other words, to back up and store files on servers that Microsoft maintains on the internet. If you have a Microsoft account, you are entitled to 5 gigabytes of free storage space on the Microsoft cloud. If you have an Office 365 subscription, you are entitled to 1,054 gigabytes (1 terabyte). Here's the big advantage of OneDrive: You can access files that you keep on the cloud from any computer connected to the internet, whether you're in Tallahassee or Timbuktu. Use one of these techniques to open the Set Up OneDrive dialog box and tell Windows 11 that you want to use OneDrive:

    • Select the OneDrive icon in the notification area located in the lower-right corner of the screen.

    • Select the Search icon on the taskbar and enter **onedrive** in the Search box; then select the OneDrive app in the search results.

If you're signed in with a Microsoft account, Windows 11 already knows your password. Skip to Step 3.

2. In the Set Up OneDrive dialog box, enter your email address and select the Sign In button. In the dialog box that appears, enter the password to your email account and select the Sign In button.

3. The next dialog box welcomes you to OneDrive or tells you where your OneDrive folder is located (which dialog box you see depends on whether you are signed in with a Microsoft or a local account). Click the Next button or Close button as necessary. You're ready to copy the folders you want to back up or store into your OneDrive folder in the Microsoft cloud.

4. Open File Explorer and copy the folders you want to back up or store into the OneDrive folder. As shown in **Figure 16-5**, this folder appears in the navigation pane on the left side of the File Explorer window. The folder will have a cloud icon likely followed by your name and `Personal`. Don't let appearances fool you. Although the OneDrive folder appears alongside the other folders in the navigation pane, that folder lives in the Microsoft cloud, not on your computer. Folders and files on OneDrive have a status icon to let you know where those files are located. A cloud icon means the files are on the internet and accessible only if you're connected to the internet. A green check mark means the files are located on your computer. (Refer to **Figure 16-5**.)

Chapter 15 explains how to copy and move files with File Explorer. As well, it explains how to create and save files.

5. In File Explorer, open one of the folders on your computer that you copied to OneDrive, create a new file, and save the new file under the name **Sync** in the folder you opened.

6. In File Explorer, select the OneDrive folder and then, in OneDrive, open the folder with the same name as the folder you opened in Step 5. You see the Sync file on OneDrive. When you save a file in a folder that is also kept on OneDrive, a copy of the file is made to OneDrive automatically. Microsoft calls this *syncing* (for synchronizing). Thanks to syncing, you don't have to copy files to OneDrive on your own because the copies are made automatically.

OneDrive folder   **Status icons**

FIGURE 16-5

TIP

To see which folders from your computer are synced to folders in OneDrive, select the OneDrive icon in the notification area, choose the Help & Settings icon on the dialog box (the icon looks like a gear), and then choose Settings in the pop-out menu. The Microsoft OneDrive dialog box appears. On the Account tab, select the Choose Folders button. The Choose Folders dialog box appears, as shown in **Figure 16-6**. You can deselect a folder in this dialog box to prevent OneDrive from syncing a folder on your computer to its counterpart folder on OneDrive. Deselect a folder if you don't care to back up its contents on OneDrive.

7. Start the Edge browser and go to the OneDrive online website at this address: onedrive.live.com. If necessary, enter your password. You see the folders from your computer that you store on OneDrive, as shown in **Figure 16-7**. You can manage your files and folders by starting here. For example, you can delete, move, and download files and folders.

TIP

Chapter 6 shows how to use Edge, the official web browser of Windows 11.

FIGURE 16-6

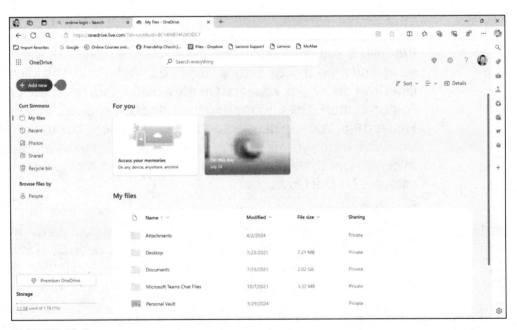

FIGURE 16-7

Reset a Misbehaving Computer

1. Glitch happens. The computer misbehaves, a program crashes, or the machine becomes unexpectedly slow. If your computer is misbehaving, try resetting it. Select the Search icon on the taskbar and type **settings**. Select the Settings app in the search results. Under System, scroll down and select Recovery (see **Figure 16-8**).

TIP

Before you reset your PC, see Chapter 13 for information about updating and maintaining Windows 11. Updating Windows may resolve some problems.

TIP

The Reset function should leave your data alone and unchanged. However, make sure you have used Windows Backup to protect your files and settings. Better safe than sorry.

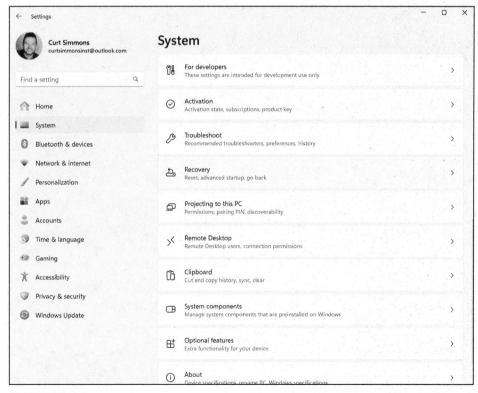

FIGURE 16-8

2. Under Reset This PC, select the Reset PC button, as shown in **Figure 16-9**.

TIP

Before choosing the reset option, try the Fix problems Without Resetting Your PC option first (refer to **Figure 16-9**). This action may fix the PC's problems much faster.

TIP

The Reset function doesn't remove apps installed through the Microsoft Store but does remove any apps you installed any other way. This safety feature is based on the assumption that something you installed from some other source is causing a problem. Be certain that you either don't need a desktop app or that you have the materials necessary to reinstall a desktop app, such as Microsoft Office. Windows 11 will create a file on the desktop after the fact, identifying the programs it removed.

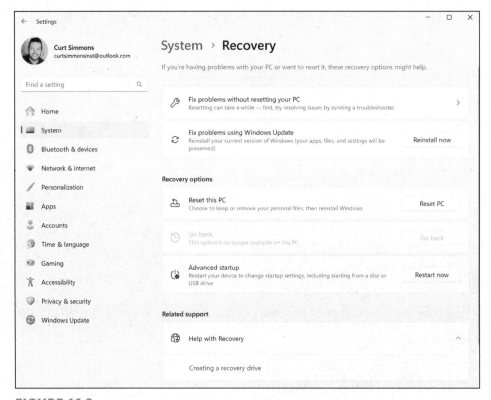

FIGURE 16-9

3. In the Choose an Option dialog box, select Keep My Files. (Or select Cancel, if you're just exploring this feature and don't want to continue with it.)

4. Reset runs, and your computer will restart at least once. When the reset process is complete, the Lock screen appears. Sign in as usual. If you see a file named Removed Apps on the desktop, double-click or double-tap it to open that file in your browser. The removed apps are listed. If you're aware that one of these apps created a problem, don't reinstall it.

Don't be intimidated by the Reset function — it's easy, quick, and worthwhile if it makes a problem computer run better.

TIP

Recovering a PC and Your Files

1. Maybe your PC was destroyed by an extra large glass of spilled iced tea, or maybe your extra-large dog decided to chew up your laptop. Either way, by using Windows Backup and OneDrive, you have nothing to worry about in terms of your files; they are all safely stowed on the internet. To access them on your newly fixed or replaced computer, you'll be prompted to log in with your Microsoft account.

2. After you log in, Windows 11 sees that you have a backup from your previous computer. Windows 11 asks whether you want to use that backup. Click Yes and then simply follow the onscreen prompts, and all your data and settings will be downloaded and applied to your new or repaired computer.

3. Next, click the OneDrive icon in the notification area and log in to OneDrive if you're not logged in already. Go to File Explorer, select the OneDrive icon on the left, and you'll see all your files stored safely on the internet.

If you have a catastrophic computer failure or loss, you can also get help with restoring all your files from support.microsoft.com. It's not a bad idea to get help if you're not sure what to do!

TIP

Index

About the Author

Curt Simmons is the best-selling author of nearly 100 technology books on a variety of topics, including *Drone Piloting For Dummies*. He is also a courseware developer focusing on Microsoft products and photography. When Curt is not writing or teaching, he enjoys numerous outdoor activities such as fishing, gardening, and flying his drone in beautiful locations around the world. He's also continuously restoring his 125-year-old Victorian home. He lives in Texas with his wife, Dawn, and two Sphynx cats.

Dedication

As always, for Dawn.

Author's Acknowledgments

I would like to thank Steven Hayes at Wiley for giving me the opportunity to write this book and Susan Christophersen for editing it. Thanks as well go to Ryan Williams, the technical editor, who made sure all instructions were accurate.

Publisher's Acknowledgments

Executive Editor: Steven Hayes

Project Manager and Copy Editor: Susan Christophersen

Technical Editor: Ryan Williams

Production Editor: Tamilmani Varadharaj

Cover Image: © blackCAT/Getty Images

Take dummies with you everywhere you go!

Whether you are excited about e-books, want more from the web, must have your mobile apps, or are swept up in social media, dummies makes everything easier.

Find us online!

dummies.com

Leverage the power

Dummies is the global leader in the reference category and one of the most trusted and highly regarded brands in the world. No longer just focused on books, customers now have access to the dummies content they need in the format they want. Together we'll craft a solution that engages your customers, stands out from the competition, and helps you meet your goals.

Advertising & Sponsorships

Connect with an engaged audience on a powerful multimedia site, and position your message alongside expert how-to content. Dummies.com is a one-stop shop for free, online information and know-how curated by a team of experts.

- Targeted ads
- Video
- Email Marketing
- Microsites
- Sweepstakes sponsorship

20 MILLION PAGE VIEWS EVERY SINGLE MONTH

15 MILLION UNIQUE VISITORS PER MONTH

43% OF ALL VISITORS ACCESS THE SITE VIA THEIR MOBILE DEVICES

700,000 NEWSLETTER SUBSCRIPTIONS TO THE INBOXES OF

300,000 UNIQUE INDIVIDUALS EVERY WEEK

# of dummies

Custom Publishing

Reach a global audience in any language by creating a solution that will differentiate you from competitors, amplify your message, and encourage customers to make a buying decision.

- Apps
- Books
- eBooks
- Video
- Audio
- Webinars

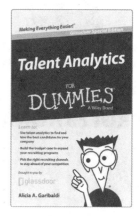

Brand Licensing & Content

Leverage the strength of the world's most popular reference brand to reach new audiences and channels of distribution.

For more information, visit **dummies.com/biz**

PERSONAL ENRICHMENT

9781119187790
USA $26.00
CAN $31.99
UK £19.99

9781119179030
USA $21.99
CAN $25.99
UK £16.99

9781119293354
USA $24.99
CAN $29.99
UK £17.99

9781119293347
USA $22.99
CAN $27.99
UK £16.99

9781119310068
USA $22.99
CAN $27.99
UK £16.99

9781119235606
USA $24.99
CAN $29.99
UK £17.99

9781119251163
USA $24.99
CAN $29.99
UK £17.99

9781119235491
USA $26.99
CAN $31.99
UK £19.99

9781119279952
USA $24.99
CAN $29.99
UK £17.99

9781119283133
USA $24.99
CAN $29.99
UK £17.99

9781119287117
USA $24.99
CAN $29.99
UK £16.99

9781119130246
USA $22.99
CAN $27.99
UK £16.99

PROFESSIONAL DEVELOPMENT

9781119311041
USA $24.99
CAN $29.99
UK £17.99

9781119255796
USA $39.99
CAN $47.99
UK £27.99

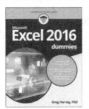
9781119293439
USA $26.99
CAN $31.99
UK £19.99

9781119281467
USA $26.99
CAN $31.99
UK £19.99

9781119280651
USA $29.99
CAN $35.99
UK £21.99

9781119251132
USA $24.99
CAN $29.99
UK £17.99

9781119310563
USA $34.00
CAN $41.99
UK £24.99

9781119181705
USA $29.99
CAN $35.99
UK £21.99

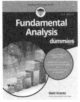
9781119263593
USA $26.99
CAN $31.99
UK £19.99

9781119257769
USA $29.99
CAN $35.99
UK £21.99

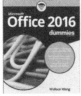
9781119293477
USA $26.99
CAN $31.99
UK £19.99

9781119265313
USA $24.99
CAN $29.99
UK £17.99

9781119239314
USA $29.99
CAN $35.99
UK £21.99

9781119293323
USA $29.99
CAN $35.99
UK £21.99

dummies.com

dummies®
A Wiley Brand

Learning Made Easy

ACADEMIC

9781119293576
USA $19.99
CAN $23.99
UK £15.99

9781119293637
USA $19.99
CAN $23.99
UK £15.99

9781119293491
USA $19.99
CAN $23.99
UK £15.99

9781119293460
USA $19.99
CAN $23.99
UK £15.99

9781119293590
USA $19.99
CAN $23.99
UK £15.99

9781119215844
USA $26.99
CAN $31.99
UK £19.99

9781119293378
USA $22.99
CAN $27.99
UK £16.99

9781119293521
USA $19.99
CAN $23.99
UK £15.99

9781119239178
USA $18.99
CAN $22.99
UK £14.99

9781119263883
USA $26.99
CAN $31.99
UK £19.99

Available Everywhere Books Are Sold

dummies.com

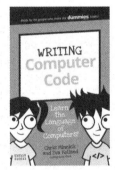